The
Lost Rites and Rituals of Freemasonry

The Lost Rites and Rituals of Freemasonry

Dr David Harrison

DEDICATION
For Helen and Samantha

Front cover and title page: Lights. *David Harrison*

All photographs taken by Dr David Harrison unless otherwise stated.

Abbreviations

AQC *Transactions of the Ars Quatuor Coronatorum*
GCR *The Grand College of Rites*
JWMT *Journal of the Western Mystery Tradition*
MAMR *Manchester Association for Masonic Research*
SRJ *Scottish Rite Journal*
SRRS *Scottish Rite Research Society*
UGLE *The United Grand Lodge of England*

First published 2017

ISBN 978 0 85318 541 3

Published by Lewis Masonic

an imprint of Ian Allan Publishing Ltd, Addlestone, Surrey KT15 2SF.

Printed in England.

Visit the Lewis Masonic website at www.lewismasonic.co.uk

Picture Credits
Every effort has been made to identify and correctly attribute photographic credits. Should any error have occurred this is entirely unintentional.

Contents

About the Author

Dr David Harrison is a UK based Masonic historian who has so far written nine books on the history of English Freemasonry and has contributed many papers and articles on the subject to various journals and magazines, such as the *AQC*, *Philalethes Journal*, the UK based *Freemasonry Today*, *MQ Magazine*, *The Square*, the US based *Knight Templar Magazine* and the *Masonic Journal*. Harrison has also appeared on TV and radio discussing his work. Having gained his PhD from the University of Liverpool in 2008, which focused on the development of English Freemasonry, the thesis was subsequently published in March 2009 entitled *The Genesis of Freemasonry* by Lewis Masonic. The work became a best seller and is now on its third edition. Harrison's other works include *The Transformation of Freemasonry* published by Arima Publishing in 2010, the *Liverpool Masonic Rebellion and the Wigan Grand Lodge* also published by Arima in 2012, *A Quick Guide to Freemasonry* which was published by Lewis Masonic in 2013, an examination of the *York Grand Lodge* published in 2014, *Freemasonry and Fraternal Societies* published in 2015, *The City of York: A Masonic Guide* published in 2016, and a biography on 19th century Liverpool philanthropist *Christopher Rawdon* which was published in the same year. Harrison regularly gives lectures on many aspects of Masonic history to lodges and conferences all over the world and is a member of the Lodge of Lights No. 148 in the West Lancashire Province under the United Grand Lodge of England. He is also an advisor for the Provincial Ambassador scheme.

Acknowledgements

In the research and writing of this book I would like to thank a host of people; first and foremost I would like to thank Masonic historian John Belton (member of Quatuor Coronati Lodge) for his encouragement, his peer review of the book and his never ending supply of old editions of *AQC* which became invaluable as a source for referencing the many papers that have been dedicated to the lost rites and occult revivalists. I would also like to especially thank Arturo de Hoyos (Supreme Council 33° S.J.) for his advice, and who, along with Josef Wages (co-author of The Secret School of Wisdom) supplied me with many translated rituals for the various rites. I would also like to thank Martin Cherry of the Library and Museum of Freemasonry, Jack Parker of the Liverpool Lodge No. 1547, Enea Kujtim Gjonaj for his information on modern day Elus Coens and Bavarian Illuminati practices, and a thank you also to Masonic authors PD Newman and Philip Carter for their ideas, which they allowed me to discuss and explore in the book. I would also like to thank Andrew Halton for developing my ideas in his excellent design for the cover of the book, and finally I would like to thank friends and family, and all at Lewis Masonic for their continued support, especially Martin Faulks and Alan Butcher.

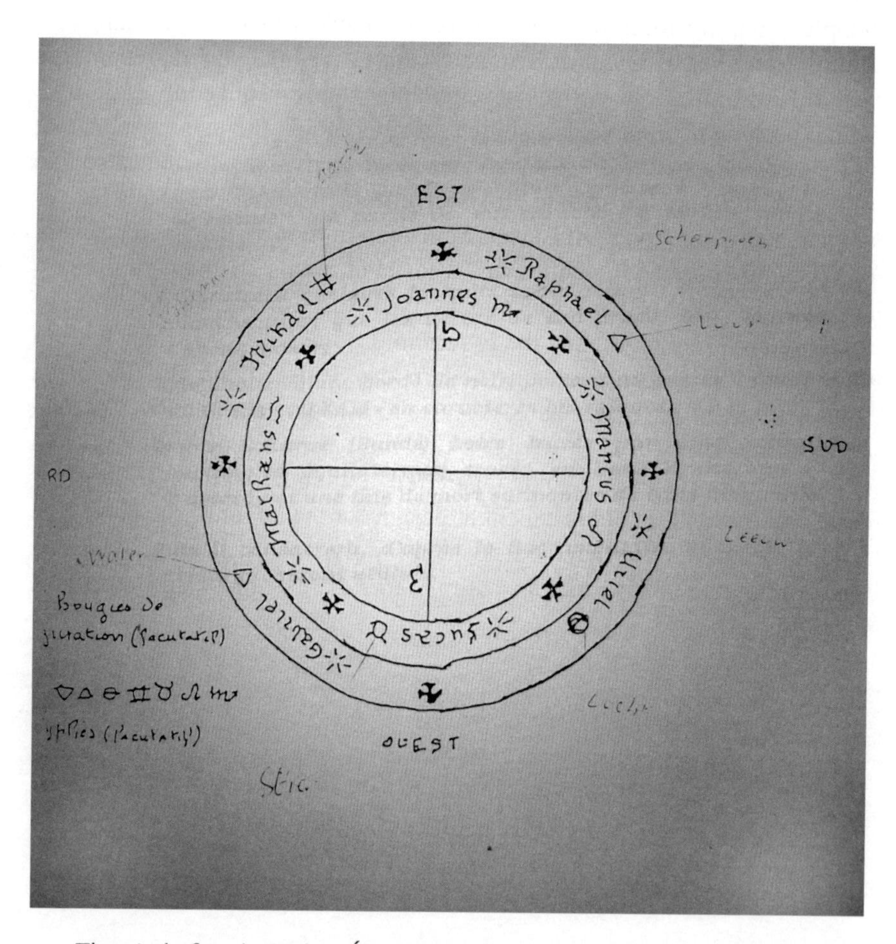

The circle for *du Maître Élu Cohen*. The drawing was included in a collection of papers given to the author by a member of the modern version of the Order.

Foreword

In most countries of the world, the newly initiated Freemason understands that Craft Masonry, under the authority of the Grand Lodges, consists of but three degrees: Entered Apprentice, Fellow Craft, and Master Mason. Soon, however, one learns that there are other 'high degrees,' which may, or may not, be acknowledged by the Grand Lodge. Some of the most popular of these additional degrees include the Mark Master Mason, the Holy Royal Arch, the Knight of Malta, and the Knight of Templar. If one looks further, one discovers the Allied Masonic Degrees, the Ancient and Accepted (Scottish) Rite, and others. Some of the degrees are traditional to Masonic themes, such as the rebuilding of Solomon's temple, or a quest to reconquer the Holy Land. Others are much more esoteric, and may include discussions of alchemy and kabbalah. The common element is that they require Masonic membership as a prerequisite to joining. Although nobody knows exactly how many Masonic degrees have been created, Ray V. Denslow examined the texts of more than two thousand while preparing his book *Masonic Rites and Degrees* (1955). The book, which is essentially a catalogue with brief descriptions, is useful for learning which degrees belonged to a given rite, although it provides very little history and even less of a description.

> "The word 'rite', from the Latin *ritus,* is cognate with the Greek αριθμός [*arithmos*]*, meaning* 'number'. In masonic as in liturgical use, the word 'rite' refers to an event, or sequence of events, which govern(s) the prescribed actions or practices of a ceremony or organized group. There are two main types of rites in Freemasonry: (1) a procedure with a symbolic or defining nature, such as the rites of circumambulation, discalceation, or investiture, which may be grouped to form a larger ceremony (or degree), and (2) the linking of masonic degrees, for initiation or instruction, under administrative or governmental authority….
>
> "As Freemasonry spread throughout the world modifications were gradually introduced to its rituals at local levels. The basic themes of the three primary degrees have remained relatively uniform, as have the modes of recognition (although 'significant

> words' may be reordered). However, different locales retained or eliminated some practices and procedures while developing new ones. Just as the evolution of language and customs creates new cultures among peoples, so have masonic practices evolved unique characteristics, or expressions of ritual, which allow them to be classified as separate Rites. In a general sense a Rite is any number of degrees grouped together. A Rite may be compared with a staircase, which is comprised of individual steps. The steps represent individual masonic degrees, whereas the staircase *as a whole* is analogous to a Rite. The degrees of a Rite will usually, although not always, have a numerical designation or fixed position on a calendar or schedule. The Rite may be further divided into sub-organisations ('lodges', 'chapters', 'councils', etc.), just as a staircase may be divided by a number of 'landings' which connect the stairs between floors. The degrees which comprise a Rite may be arranged in a particular sequence for any number of reasons, including mythology, chronology and/or tradition, or they may appear to be unrelated to each other, having been derived from various sources, or having been aggregated at different times."[1]

The study of different rites affords the Mason a much broader and deeper perspective and understanding of the Craft than is possible by limiting himself to the ritual by which he was made a Mason. One ritual may explain in great detail what is merely an incidental artefact in another, or it may retain symbols which have altogether disappeared. Thus, by examining related rituals, we gain a more complete picture of the essence of the degree. The experience is somewhat like having access to a family history which includes both ancestors and relatives.

We are fortunate to live in a time where access to ritual information is easier than ever. Many Masonic organisations now print their own rituals, or offer them through a Masonic supplier, such as Lewis Masonic. And, for those of us who have an interest in ritual archaeology, there are other tremendous sources available. For example, since 1932, the Grand College of Rites of the United States of America[2] has printed *Collectanea*, its official transaction. Each volume of *Collectanea* reprints the rituals of disused and irregular Masonic and quasi-Masonic organisations, for study. The collection is a virtual encyclopaedia of primary sources on disused ritual systems. The Latomia Foundation[3] is an online resource which provides its members access to digital files of dozens of ritual manuscripts and studies.

Other organisations have also contributed significantly to our understanding of Masonic ritual. The publications of Quatuor Coronati Lodge 2076 (London, United Grand Lodge of England), the Supreme Council, 33°, Southern Jurisdiction (United States), the Grand Orient of France, and others, have all produced scholarly works.

The book you are now holding, however, is long overdue. David Harrison has produced a kind of companion volume to the above resources, a guidebook to many of the 'lost' Masonic rites, some of which played significant roles in our history. Bro. Harrison's book is not an autopsy of dead Rites, not a dry, academic text. It provides extracts from the rituals themselves, and offers interesting insights into their nature, as well as a bit of history to place them within context. It's a book which should be kept alongside one's Masonic encyclopaedia, or ritual collection. I've enjoyed reading it, and I invite you to do the same.

Arturo de Hoyos, 33°, Grand Cross, K.Y.C.H.
Grand Archivist and Grand Historian
Supreme Council, 33°, Southern Jurisdiction
Grand Archivist, Premiere Knight Grand Cross
Grand College of Rites of the United States of America

Introduction

With the introduction of a third degree in the mid-1720s with its powerful theatrical portrayal of the Hiramic legend and its embedded theme of the search for lost knowledge, other degrees soon followed as Freemasons wished to explore further grades within the framework of Masonry, most notably the Royal Arch, which appeared by the 1740s and the Knight Templar degree that began to appear slightly later. On the Continent in countries such as France and Germany, it was not long before more exotic and extravagant Masonic rites began to be practiced; rites that presented a number of colourful degrees that gave the Freemason an extended pathway to explore, creating a Masonic journey of discovery and exaltation. Some of these rites had a political element, especially with the Jacobite threat and the intrigue that this created. Other rites had a more magical tone, which offered the Freemason a more mystical and empowered experience, presenting a pathway to God himself.

In the mid-late eighteenth century, these rites worked a common combination of seven or nine grades, being a manageable collection of *haut grades* that resounded with either Templar themes, Egyptian ideas, magical elements or even a hint of all three. It seemed some Masons wanted more, and more was certainly what they got; during latter half of the eighteenth century, the Rite of Perfection offered 25 degrees, and by the early nineteenth century, the Rite of Memphis and Rite of Misraïm offered even more. Indeed, an explosion of degrees occurred that presented a deeper progression within the Masonic framework, the grades encompassing an array of themes, symbolism and esotericism.

This book will examine the history and evolution of these rites, some of which were indeed quite bizarre. There are countless rites that emerged during the eighteenth century, including some long lost rites such as the mysterious Rite of Zinnendorf, the Rite de Elus Coens, the Rite of the Black Eagle, the Rite of Seven Degrees and Cagliostro's Egyptian Rite. Some of these rites became disused after a few years, others merged with other rites or evolved into degrees or grades that are practiced today, such as the Rose Croix Degree. The Scottish Rite will be discussed as an Order that evolved from a more obscure European Rite and survived to become one of the most famous and enduring rites, a rite that was also of interest to some English Masons of the nineteenth century who were evidently interested in higher degrees such as Liverpool Masonic rebel Michael Alexander Gage and Dr George Oliver. A particular collection of lost English rituals of special interest are the *Old Lancashire Rituals* which were written down by John Yarker in 1865 after visiting a Lancashire based lodge, and these will be examined extensively for the first time. Indeed the many varied Craft rituals that emerged in England after the union will be looked at, and how some of them are in danger of being lost, will be discussed.

Certain lost rites have somewhat obscure origins and have consisted of some rather bizarre ceremonies, such as Cagliostro's Egyptian Rite, which existed in the later eighteenth century and, according to recent study, may have consisted of using the root of a certain genus of acacia plant during the ritual to produce a potentially psychoactive experience. Another rather bizarre ceremony is said to a have occurred during the Rite of Egyptian Priests, a Para-Masonic ritual that took place in Germany in the 1760s-1790s and featured the theatrical killing of Egyptian and Greek Gods within the ritual. Other rites indulged in a more magical experience, such as the Order of the Gold and Rosy Cross which took place in Germany during the 1750s. This particular rite promoted the use of alchemy and took its teachings down a more esoteric pathway, creating a more magical and eclectic route within the Masonic framework. All of these more curious lost rites evolved from a template of Masonic ritual, the rites becoming a way of experimenting and expanding on a theme during a time when the search for lost knowledge knew no bounds.

Indeed, this evolution of Masonic degrees will be a theme of the book; there is a rich and fascinating tapestry in regards to the development of Masonic rites, some of which can be linked together during this heady manic period for access to high degrees in the eighteenth and early nineteenth centuries. As Masonic historian Lionel Seemungal once wrote 'the surviving degrees and orders are the distilled essence of the past', the lifeblood of some of the degrees that we practice today having their origins in these lost degrees.[4] With the egos of the men behind them and a dangerous blend of politics, magic and power, Freemasonry was taken into a very experimental place, a place where we will now explore.

Part I

The
Lost Rites
and the
Search for Hidden Knowledge

Chapter 1

The Evolution of Masonic Rites

That in order to avoid all sorts of schism and disunion among Masons their hearts must be drawn to each other by an attachment, a confidence and a boundless fraternal devotion.
First Degree of Cagliostro's Egyptian Rite. [5]

...I beg of you, to give me greater enlightenment concerning this natural philosophy.
First Degree of Cagliostro's Egyptian Rite.[6]

What is the sign of an Elect Master?
Answer: To see, without being seen.
Fourth Degree, Melissino's Rite.[7]

In my book *The Genesis of Freemasonry*, I proposed how Dr Jean Theophilus Desaguliers was responsible for creating the third degree by the mid-1720s. Before this, there were two parts being performed; the Entered Apprentice and the Fellow Craft, and we have little evidence of what they were like.[8] However, we do know that these two parts were often performed at the same lodge meeting, with evidence from the early minutes of the Old York Lodge indicating how a lodge could be opened in another town especially to admit a large number of candidates, such as in Scarborough in 1705 when a lodge was opened to admit six men into the Fraternity, and in Bradford in 1713, where 18 men were recorded as being admitted.[9]

Indeed, to further support the fact that there were just two parts in Freemasonry at this time, it states in the Ancient Charges displayed in Anderson's *Constitutions* of 1723 that 'No Brother can be a Warden until he has passed the part of a Fellow Craft', indicating that the part of Fellow Craft was the senior 'grade' that allowed the Mason to take part in an Office if so desired. In the 1738 edition of the Constitutions, the wording of this particular charge had been changed to 'The Wardens are chosen from among the Master Masons', suggesting that the third degree of Master Mason had by this time been introduced and the Constitutions had to be updated. By 1730, the publication of Samuel Pritchard's exposé *Masonry Dissected*, revealed the three degree ritual, and it seemed that this new tri-gradal system became very popular indeed.[10]

The new three degree style ritual soon spread, even being referred to by Dr Francis Drake in his now famous Oration, given on St. John's Day, 27 December 1726, in the Merchant Adventurers' Hall in York, where he stated that *'three parts in four of the whole Earth might then be divided into e:p:f:c&m:m'*.[11] The themes of the third degree deeply explored the search for lost knowledge; the degree portraying the search for the lost word of God that was hidden in the architecture of Solomon's Temple. With the symbolic death of Hiram Abiff, this knowledge was lost.[12] It seemed that Freemasons soon wanted to explore deeper pathways within Masonry, leading to new ideas being developed. Chevalier Ramsey was a Jacobite Mason who had gone to France to tutor the sons of aristocrats, and in his Masonic address in 1737, he famously outlined that Freemasonry was linked to the Crusaders and Chivalric Orders. His Oration put forward that after being preserved in the British Isles, it was transported to France, and though there is no evidence that Masonry was associated in any way to the Crusaders or Chivalry, it does show that at this time there was a developing interest in Chivalric Orders in relation to Freemasonry. Though Ramsey did not set out any plans for new Chivalric Masonic Orders in his Oration his address certainly assisted to inspire them.[13]

In 1733, there appears to have been a 'Scotts Masons Lodge' meeting at the Devil Tavern in London, with a 'Scotch Master' being made in Bath in the south-west of England in 1746.[14] According to Masonic historian John Belton, the Scots degree seemed to include the discovery in a vault of the long lost word, and Scots Crusaders working with a sword in one hand and a trowel in the other, but in the time of Zerubbabel instead of the Crusades.[15] This Scots Masters theme will be discussed later, as it was an idea that filtered into some of the rites that occurred on the Continent. Another enigmatic early grade was that of Harodim, which was mentioned by Bro. Joseph Laycock in an Oration, published in Newcastle in 1736, the Harodim Workings connected to the old Swalwell Lodge in Durham.[16] The possible first hints of a mysterious ritual that is reminiscent of our modern day Royal Arch emerged by 1740, though the authenticity of the source itself has been debated; the Rite Ancien de Bouillon gives an early mention of a plate of gold, and refer to a symbol that consisted of a double triangle within a circle and the tetragrammaton in the centre.[17] In 1746, the Freemason John Coustos published an account of his torture by the Inquisition, whereby he admitted his Masonic activities and described a part of the ritual which was remarkably similar to the Royal Arch, namely the finding of a tablet of bronze amongst the ruins of the Temple.[18] Coustos had been made a Mason in London but had left for Portugal in 1743, where he had continued to be an active Freemason. He was subsequently arrested and tortured, his suffering revealing the fragments of an early secret ritual. Today in the Royal Arch ritual in England, the long lost name of God is discovered on the plate of gold within the ruins of the first Temple, something that was alluded to in Richard Carlile's Royal Arch ritual which was compiled from various sources in the early nineteenth century.

There are further mentions of the Royal Arch at this time; a report in Faulkner's Dublin Journal gives details of a procession on St John's Day in 1743 at Youghal in Ireland, referring to 'the Royall Arch carried by two Excellent Masons'. The following year, Dublin based Fifield Dassigny wrote in his *Serious and Impartial Enquiry into the Cause of the Present Decay of Free-Masonry in the Kingdom of Ireland*, of how 'a certain propagator of a false system some few years ago in this city who imposed upon several very worthy men under a pretence of being a Master of the Royal Arch, which he asserted he had brought with him from the city of York...' Dassigny continues to provide us with a glimpse behind the veil, writing that the Royal Arch was 'an organised body of men who have passed the Chair and given undeniable proofs of their skill', adding that some brethren did not like 'such a secret ceremony being kept from those who had taken the usual degrees'. This seems to imply that the Royal Arch ritual was relatively new and was indeed a further degree to be experienced by certain Masons; a pathway for a select few.[19]

The Craft rituals at this time were far from standardised and this created liberty to explore new stories, to create sequels to the Hiramic legend and the building of the Temple. All this was happening during a time when English Freemasonry became split and was arguing over how the Royal Arch should fit into the system. That is not to say that English Freemasons were not interested in further degrees, on the contrary, it was during this fertile period that the Knights Templar was being practiced and, by the later eighteenth century, the Mark Degree was firmly capturing the English Masonic mind. As we shall see later, there were rites and localised ritualistic pathways that took hold and developed in England. There were three Grand Lodges operating in England during the latter half of the eighteenth century; the Moderns, the Antients and the Grand Lodge of all England held at York, and all three had a different style of administration and a different system of ritual. The Moderns seemed uncomfortable with the Royal Arch, whereas the Antients embraced it as an additional degree. The York Grand Lodge went even further and by the 1770s were practicing five degrees; the three Craft degrees, the Royal Arch as a fourth and the Knights Templar as a fifth. It seemed some Masons wanted more.[20]

Early Obscure Rites

Masonic writer Arthur Edward Waite discusses a number of obscure rites that possibly developed during the early eighteenth century in his *New Encyclopaedia of Freemasonry*, rites that have an element of mystery surrounding them, were in some cases there is some doubt as to when they were actually founded or when they ceased working. There were rites such as the Order of the Palladium, which Waite mentions was founded in Paris in 1737,[21] the Order of Amazons which allowed both sexes as members and was founded in South America in 1740[22] and the Order of Xerophagists, which Waite states was founded in Italy in 1748.[23] There was the Order of African Architects which Waite puts forward as 'exceedingly doubtful' as being founded in 1756, but was probably founded later in 1765 and ended in 1806.[24] The Rite of the Sublime Elects of Truth has a doubtful foundation date of 1776, the same year being given for the foundation of the Rite Ecossais Philosophique.[25] Other obscure rites include the Rite of the Black Eagle,[26] the Persian Rite,[27] and the Order of Jerusalem.[28]

The Order of Jerusalem, according to Waite, was founded in North America in 1791, had eight degrees, was an association of alchemists and had a connection to the Rite of Chastanier, having spread to Germany, England, Holland and Russia, though Waite suggests that 'the whole story is doubtful'.[29] The Persian Rite is another rite with an obscure history; Waite suggesting it may have been established at Erzurum in Turkey in 1818, but appeared in Paris a year later and worked seven degrees which contained three classes. The first class consisted of three degrees that in essence were similar to Craft Masonry; *Listening Apprentice*, *Fellow Craft Adept* and *Master*, the second class consisted of the fourth degree entitled *Architect of All Rites* and a fifth degree named *Knight of Eclecticism and Truth*, the third class concluded the rite and included a sixth degree entitled *Master*

Good Shepherd and a seventh and final degree called *Venerable Grand Elect*. However, Waite concludes that despite being able to name its degree system, there is no evidence that the rite existed at all.[30]

The Rite of Adonhiramite (sometimes referred to as Adoniramite) is another lesser known eighteenth century rite that had twelve degrees, its creation being attributed by nineteenth century French Masonic author Jean Baptiste Marie Ragon to Baron de Tschoudy.[31] However, according to Masonic scholar and ritual specialist Arturo de Hoyos, the system is still worked in Brazil, so technically it is not lost.[32] The Rose Croix appears here as it does in many of these rites, the Christian imagery and symbolism forming a mystical conclusion to a collection of rituals that are similar to other rites that explore the Scottish Master degree, which is featured here as the tenth degree. There were a number of rites that were less obscure and went on to influence other rites and degrees, some evolving and inspiring later Orders, and it is these rites that we shall examine next.

Jacobite and Templar Themes of the Early Rites

The eighteenth century was certainly a breeding ground for Masonic ritual as new ideas evolved and expanded to create many bizarre rites. Indeed, during this fertile era of enlightenment, more and more exotic rites began to be created at an exceptional rate, especially on the European Continent. One such early rite according to John Yarker writing in his *Arcane Schools*, was called the *Vielle Bru*, or Faithful Scots, based at Toulouse, at Montpelier and at Marseilles, constituted by Sir Samuel Lockhart between 1743-1751. Yarker describes how the rite 'drew on the legends of the old operative Guilds and did not proceed in its instruction beyond the 2nd temple'. It was constructed of nine degrees, the last of which was curiously named *Menatzchim* or *Perfects*. A similar rite soon emerged in Paris called the Knights of the East in 1751, and like the Vielle Bru, was said by Yarker to have explored similar Scottish and themes that perhaps reflected the interest in Jacobite ideas.[33]

Another early rite was the Chapter of Clermont, which featured six degrees and was founded in France in 1754 by Chevalier de Bonneville.[34] Despite it only lasting for around four years, it was an early attempt at exploring *haut grades* that had a Templar theme.[35] The Chapter was said to have included the first three Craft degrees, the fourth being called *Maitre Ecossais* (Scotch Master), the fifth being *Maitre Eleu* (Master Elect or Knight of the Eagle), the sixth degree *Maitre Illustre* (Illustrious Master or

Knight of the Holy Sepulchre), and the seventh and final degree being named *Maitre Sublime* (Sublime Master and Knight of God). Yarker comments on how the higher degrees of the Chapter conveyed 'Solomon's revenge' on the murderers of Hiram, the jewel of the *Maitre Illustre* grade being a dagger stuck into a skull.[36] There was indeed a strong desire to extend the themes explored in the Craft rituals, and there were plenty of charismatic characters that were eager to create or promote new Orders and Grades based on the continuation of the themes for the search for lost knowledge.

Baron von Hund and the Rite of Strict Observance

One such charismatic individual was Baron Karl Gotthelf von Hund, who in around 1754 founded the Rite of Strict Observance in Germany.[37] Baron von Hund had put forward that he had been initiated into a mysterious Masonic Order of the Temple in Paris in 1742 and that his secret knowledge had been gained from 'unknown superiors'.[38] The Rite of Strict Observance became a rather popular rite, spreading to many other European countries such as Switzerland, Holland, Denmark and Russia, and included a tantalising seven degrees, offering the philosophy of progression to willing Masons who desired more.[39]

These seven degrees, according to the transcription of the Schröder rituals[40] by Alain Bernheim and Arturo de Hoyos, included the first Craft degrees of *Apprentice*, *Fellow* and *Master Mason*, followed by *Scots Master*, *Secular Novice*, *Knight*, and finally *Lay Brother*.[41] The three Craft rituals are recognisable to any Mason, but nonetheless have stark differences, such as in the Master Mason degree which features a 'Cassia branch' instead of the Acacia sprig we know of today.[42] A collection of Catechisms are presented that seem quite unusual in certain contexts, and it appears that the rituals evolved down a very different path, though still retained the essence of the first three degrees. The rite was Templar orientated, its Chivalric content and the mystery that surrounds its supposed Jacobite origin still divides Masonic historians today. The translations by Bernheim and de Hoyos in discussing the 'Extracts From the History of the Order' present a story of how a number of Templars fled persecution in France in 1311 and arrived in Scotland, clothed as Masons. According to the story, once in Scotland, the Order continued with the 'usages of Masonry…chosen to preserve the memory…' and that 'nobody was admitted a Scots Master, other than a child of the Order…'[43] The rite in celebrating Scotland and its secret Templar heritage, seems to echo the Chivalric ideas presented in the Oration of Chevalier Ramsey, something that was also mirrored in von Hund's suggestion of a mysterious Jacobite source for the system.[44]

Indeed, Baron von Hund's undoing was the mysterious origins of the rite, and being unable to present any tangible proof of his 'unknown superiors', a result of which his story became untenable and his reputation damaged. He died in 1776 in much-reduced circumstances. At the convent of Wilhelmsbad in 1782, von Hund's rite quickly unravelled as a collection of delegates renounced the unproven Templar origins, they discarded the myth and a complete re-working of the ritual took place, ending the practice of von Hund's Rite of Strict Observance. Some Masonic writers, such as Waite, have made reference of the supposed Jacobite origins of von Hund's rite; in Paris, von Hund believed he came into contact with a certain Knight of the Red Feather, whose identity was never revealed, but von Hund believed was none other than the Young Pretender Charles Edward Stuart. Waite was of the opinion that von Hund was mistaken or deceived, but either way, the Baron maintained his story until his death and the Rite of Strict Observance was, for a short while, one of the most progressive rites in Europe during the eighteenth century.[45] Despite the end of the practice of von Hund's Rite of Strict Observance, its restructuring by Jean-Baptiste Willermoz led to the birth of the Rectified Scottish Rite, which will be discussed later in more depth. The Rite of Strict Observance also became an influence on the formation of the Rite of the Philalethes,[46] and the Swedish Rite, which is still worked in Sweden today.

The Rite of Philalethes

The Rite of Philalethes, as Waite most philosophically puts it, was 'among the several claimants to a general reformation of Masonry'.[47] It was founded in 1773 by, amongst others, the prominent French Mason Charles Pierre-Paul Savalette de Langes, and was a rather eclectic mixture of grades, being influenced by the Rite of Strict Observance and the Rite de Elus Coens (Rite of the Elect Priesthood). It gained a distinguished membership and was central in organising the famed Convention of Paris in 1784, which fervently discussed 'the true nature of Masonic science'. Despite having an illustrious membership and being quite progressive in nature, the rite seems to have collapsed after the death of Savalette de Langes in 1797, and was thus relatively short lived. Its twelve grades included the three Craft degrees of *Entered Apprentice*, *Fellow Craft* and *Master Mason*, followed by *Elect*, *Scottish Master*, *Knight of the East*, *Rose Croix*, *Knight of the Temple*, *Unknown Philosopher*, *Sublime Philosopher*, *Initiate*, and finally *Philalethes*.[48] The development of this high-grade style of Freemasonry became entwined with the egos of mystics, charismatic gentlemen and the fashions of Freemasonry on the Continent, not to mention the politics of the day, and it seems that each rite that was established was presenting what they believed was the correct form of Masonry.

Martinez de Pasqually and the Rite de Elus Coens

Martinez de Pasqually established his Rite de Elus Coens (or the Rite of the Elect Priesthood) at Toulouse in 1760. Though there is some confusion over the exact structure of the grades, according to Waite the rite reportedly had a possible nine degrees divided into three divisions; these included the Porch, which were basically the three Craft degrees that included *Apprentice*, *Companion* and *Particular Master*; the Temple, which consisted of 'Priestly' degrees that included *Grand Elect Master*, *Apprentice Priest*, *Companion Priest*; and the Shrine, which became more magical, with *Master Priest*, *Grand Master Architect*, and, according to J.M. Ragon the final grade was *Knight Commander*, which Papus later identified as a Rose Croix degree.[49]

John Yarker, in his *Arcane Schools*, mentions a curious charter or patent that was issued by none other than Charles Stuart on 20 May 1738, which gave the father of Martinez de Pasqually permission to create lodges for the Rite de Elus Coens. There are obvious difficulties with a document such as this; Yarker mentions that Charles Stuart – the Bonnie Prince Charlie of history – is described in the document as King of Scotland, Ireland and England, and Grand Master of All Lodges on the face of the earth.[50] At the time the document was supposedly written, the Bonnie Prince was only 17 and it was his father - the old pretender James III - who claimed the three crowns at this point. Despite its questionable authenticity, the document was mentioned over a century ago by Yarker and is still valued by Elus Coen groups that exist today.[51] The charter undoubtedly reminds one of Baron von Hund's 'unknown superiors' and how the Bonnie Prince was associated with the Knight of the Red Feather. There was certainly a fashion for Masonic charters in the name of the Bonnie Prince during this time; Yarker also refers to a certain Lord de Berkley who, on 14 February 1747, granted a charter for the Rose Croix to the Lodge 'Jacobite Scots' at Arras

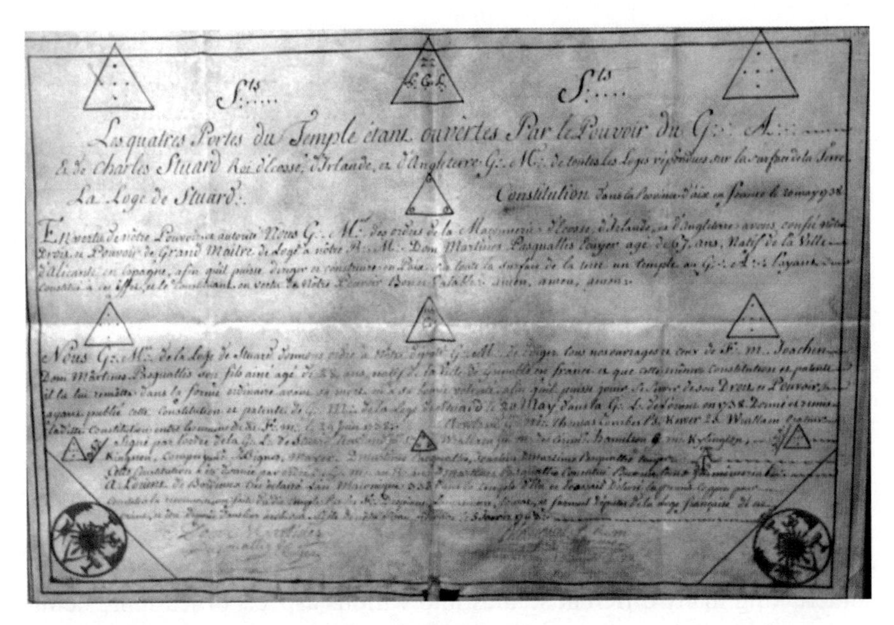
S:....

S:....

Les quatres Portes du Temple étant ouvertes Par le Pouvoir du G:. A:.

Et de Charles Stuard Roi d'Ecosse, d'Irlande, et d'Angleterre G:. M:. de toutes les Loges répandues sur la surface de la Terre

La Loge de Stuard:.

Constitution

The Jacobite Charter of the Rite de Elus Coens, referred to by John Yarker in his Arcane Schools. According to Ben Williams who kindly supplied the photograph, the Charter was lost to the Russians at the end of World War II and has recently been found among a cache of Masonic memorabilia. It has now been returned to a private collector among the Friends of Martinez de Pasqually in Bordeaux, France.

in France, Yarker indicating that there is no authenticated copy of the charter and Prince Charles Edward is sometimes referred to on the document as either 'King Pretendant' or 'substitute G.M.', depending on who was writing about it.[52] Interestingly, Yarker also commented on how women were not refused admission to the Rite de Elus Coens, which also reminds us of how both men and women could be part of Cagliostro's Egyptian Rite.

Pasqually merged esoteric doctrines based on Gnosticism and the Kabbala; in short, his version of Freemasonry blended with magic to form a unique type of rite. In this sense, the teachings of the Rite de Elus Coens enabled selected members to learn an aspect of magic that aimed to place the adept in communion with supernatural beings. Pasqually was particularly influential on Jean-Baptist Willermoz and Louis Claude de Saint-Martin, both taking his teachings in different directions. In 1772, Pasqually left France for the Caribbean to collect an inheritance and died there in 1774. The Order disintegrated after his death, and elements of the rite were absorbed into the restructured Rite of Strict Observance by Willermoz, creating the Rectified Scottish Rite. Saint-Martin took his teachings in another direction, teachings that later went on to influence Martinism. As we shall see in the next chapter, there was indeed a magical element of Pasqually's teachings that were part of the rite, teachings that purportedly allowed select members to commune directly with spiritual beings.

The Swedenborgian Rite

Emanuel Swedenborg has never been proven to be a Freemason; he was however a mystic, theologian, philosopher, scientist and inventor, whose teachings and work ultimately inspired the Swedenborg Rite. Emanuel Swedenborg was born in Stockholm in 1688, his father being a Professor of theology at Uppsala University and later Bishop of Skara. Swedenborg was a learned man; inventing flying machines, researching anatomy and undertaking many different studies into various aspects of learning, being a propagator in the search for the hidden mysteries of nature and science. It was later in life that Swedenborg had a spiritual awakening of sorts which witnessed a transition from a man of science to a mystic; a man who could talk to angels, spirits and demons, and who claimed to have received a new revelation from Jesus Christ, his teachings revealing the second coming of

Portrait of Emanuel Swedenborg by Carl Frederik von Breda. *http://www.newchurchhistory.org/articles/ceg2006b/ceg2006b.php*

Christ and the last judgment. Swedenborg died in London in 1772, and he went on to inspire eminent artists and writers such as William Blake and Thomas De Quincey,[53] as well as men of mysticism such as Louis Claude de Saint-Martin. The Swedenborgian Church, which was inspired by the writings of Swedenborg, was founded in England in 1787; the New Church movement as it was also known, growing quickly, the Church still surviving today. It was after his death that the 'Swedenborgian' Rite was developed by a Polish Count and Swedenborg enthusiast called Thaddeus Leszczy Grabianka and a certain Dom Antoine Joseph Pernety, fusing Swedenborg's mystical teachings with Masonic ideas.[54]

Dom Antoine Joseph Pernety had left the Benedictine Order and, after settling in Avignon, pursued his interests in alchemy. He then relocated to Berlin, becoming librarian to the Freemason Frederick the Great, and while there, he translated Swedenborg's works into French. It was in Berlin that Pernety met the Polish Count Grabianka, and after Pernety returned to Avignon, Grabianka joined him and together they founded the *Société des Illuminés d'Avignon* in 1786. This early Swedenborgian Rite was relatively short lived, coming to an end in the wake of the chaos brought by the French Revolution. They did however attract two English Swedenborgians of note; William Bryan and John Wright, who, in 1789 'were initiated into the mysteries of their order' and were introduced to 'the actual and personal presence of the Lord', who was conveyed by a 'majestic young man…in purple garments, seated on a throne', situated in an inner chamber 'decorated with heavenly emblems'.[55] This hints that the rite reflected the Millennialism philosophies of Swedenborg, but what the rest of the ritual was like, we can only speculate. Another Swedenborgian Rite surfaced with the occult revival of the later nineteenth century, again containing elements of Swedenborg's mystical Millennialism.[56]

The obscurity of the early version of the rite has led to a number of different presentations of its history and it has been said that the aforementioned *Société des Illuminés d'Avignon* had no connection at all to the later Swedenborgian Rite that developed in the USA, the later rite 'containing too much of American Craft Ritual'.[57] In an edition of *Collectanea* that discusses the rite, a reference traces it to London c.1784 where a certain Benedict Chastanier is mentioned regarding an Order based on the *Illuminated Theosophists*, which had been founded by him in 1767.[58] The edition then describes how the rite was revived in America in 1859 by members of the Swedenborgian New Church, and though this foundation date is suggested as being problematic, the rite was certainly in existence there in 1869, when a book was written about the Order by Samuel Beswick. Freemason and occultist John Yarker was also involved in the revived rite, being listed as Supreme Grand Master.[59] Six Grades are presented as being worked by the revived rite; the first three being the Craft degrees, the fourth was titled *Enlightened Phremason*, the fifth *Sublime Phremason*, and the sixth and final Grade *Perfect Phremason*.[60] In the final Grade, God's name is revealed and the Masonic journey is declared as complete.[61]

Yarker does touch on the Swedenborgian Rite in his *Arcane Schools*, stating that 'it consists of three elaborate and beautiful ceremonies for which the Craft is required.'[62] Although it has been affirmed that it has nothing to do with the earlier and more mysterious *Société des Illuminés d'Avignon*, the nineteenth century Swedenborgian Rite is an example of the difficulties that arise in assessing if a particular rite was actually revived or not. Without certain continuity and complete evidence of the rituals that were used, a revival or indeed, a claimed continuation of a particular rite will always be debatable.

The Rite of Zinnendorf

This particular rite was named after Johann Wilhelm Ellenberger von Zinnendorf, born in Halle in 1731. Zinnendorf was a prominent figure in Freemasonry, and in 1773 he struck a deal with the Grand Lodge of England that all lodges in Germany, with the exception of the Provincial Grand Lodge at Frankfort, would be placed under his charge, Zinnendorf effectively becoming Grand Master, a position he held until his death in 1782. The rite itself, according to Waite, had been said to be a concoction of the 'visions of Swedenborg' and the 'vestiges of Pernety's Hermetic Illuminism', though he mentions there was no evidence of this. Indeed, the arrangement of the rite reflects a certain influence from the Rite of Strict Observance; the first part was made up of the Craft or Blue Masonry with the *Apprentice* degree, followed by *Companion*, then *Master*. The second part was what Waite termed as Red Masonry, with *Écossais Apprentice and Companion*, followed by *Master Écossais*, then the third and final part was entitled Capitular Masonry, with a grade called *Favourite of St John*, followed by *Chapter of Elect Masons*.[63]

Zinnendorf's rite with its *Écossais* (Scottish) aspirations thus appears to have an influence from the Rite of Strict Observance. Zinnendorf had indeed been a member of the Strict Observance; he had been 'knighted' by von Hund in 1764, Zinnendorf becoming Master of the Three Globes Lodge in Berlin the following year. Von Hund constituted the Three Globes as a 'Scots or Directoral Lodge' in 1766, giving it the power to warrant Strict Observance lodges. However, the harmony was broken when in the November, Zinnendorf 'formally notified to Von Hund of his renunciation of the Strict Observance', and in May 1767 he resigned from the Three Globes. This gave Zinnendorf the freedom to create his own rite and to forge his ambitions that ultimately led to his negotiations with the Grand Lodge of England.[64] The rite has a marked similarity to the Swedish Rite, with some minor but equally significant variations.

Cagliostro's Egyptian Rite

Of all the Masonic rites that existed on the Continent during the eighteenth century, Count Alessandro Cagliostro's Egyptian Rite is perhaps one of the most intriguing and fascinating rite. Cagliostro himself was a man of mystery, of ego and of creativity; the exotic theatre of Freemasonry being the backdrop to portray his own unique blend of alchemy, sex and magic,

Engraving of Count Cagliostro.
https://commons.wikimedia.org/wiki/File:Alessandro_Cagliostro.jpg

a concoction that certainly appealed to the Parisian social elite of the time. Cagliostro became the romantic subject of writers such as Johann Wolfgang von Goethe and Alexandre Dumas,[65] and the romance surrounding his life seems to blur between fantasy and reality, creating an almost mythical Masonic character. For example, Cagliostro allegedly met illustrious eighteenth century personalities such as the Comte de Saint-Germain and Casanova, and Cagliostro's past was as mysterious as these two figures, the enigmatic magician being identified as Giuseppe Balsamo, an Italian forger and trickster, in a French newspaper published in London called *Courrier de l'Europe* in September 1786. He was again identified as Balsamo in a publication in 1791 by the Apostolic Chamber in Rome, outlining Cagliostro's trial, entitled *Vie de Joseph Balsamo*.[66] Trouble did seem to accompany Cagliostro wherever he went; while in France in the 1780s, Cagliostro had been implicated in the Affair of the Diamond necklace, which directly involved Marie Antoinette in a tangled web of dark intrigue, and after spending time in the Bastille, he was released and left for England, later leaving for Rome, where he was arrested for being a Freemason in 1789. After trying to escape from the Castel Sant'Angelo, Cagliostro was moved to the Fortress of San Leo, where he died soon after.

Cagliostro became such an important figure in Freemasonry at the time that he was invited to the Convention of Paris in 1784 to explain his system; a Convention that the Rite of the Philalethes had been instrumental in organising. His claims included that he could renew youth, he could conjure the apparitions of the dead, he could bestow beauty on those who submitted to his system of Hermetic medicine, and that he could make gold. In short, his rite would reveal the true hidden mysteries of nature and science, and as it became open to women, he began to attract a number of high-ranking ladies.[67] The rite itself consisted of three Craft-like degrees; that of *Apprentice*, *Companion* and *Master*, but these degrees consisted of some very interesting material. John Yarker in his *Arcane Schools*, believed that Cagliostro's ritual may have been influenced by Pasqually,[68] and the two rites did indeed share deeper magical aspects, as we shall explore in later chapters. Cagliostro continues to attract the interest of writers, perhaps due to the flamboyant nature of his life. Likewise his style of Freemasonry has also been the focus of attention, and later we will examine the supposed sexual nature of the rite and the possibility of a drug induced experience during the ceremony.

The Melissino Rite

Pyotr Ivanovich Melissino (1726-1797) was a General of the Artillery of the Russian Empire of Greek origin, and was the founder of the Melissino Rite, which was active in St Petersburg in Russia in 1765. Melissino was a prominent member of St Petersburg society, which was also a fashionable and cultural centre for the Enlightenment under Catherine the Great, Melissino becoming acquainted with the likes of Casanova, a man of high social standing who was also linked to Freemasonry.[69] Melissino's Rite comprised of seven degrees, and as Melissino was deeply interested in alchemy, alchemical, Rosicrucian and Kabbalistic references seeped into the rite, making this form of Freemasonry very attractive to the social elite of the time.[70] Melissino was also said to have been one of the 'most faithful followers' of Cagliostro, and as we shall see in a later chapter, there are similarities in certain parts of the rituals.[71]

The seven degrees of the rite included the first three Craft degrees of *Entered Apprentice*, *Fellow-Craft* and *Master Mason*, then continued the Hiramic legend with a fourth degree called the *Dark Vault*, with a narrative of the search for the grave of Hiram and how nine Master Masons where selected for the search. The fifth degree of *Scottish Master* is reminiscent of the Scots Master degree of the Rite of Strict Observance, the degree being Chivalric in nature, putting forward how a group of Master Masons carried away the body of Hiram and the treasure of the Temple to Scotland where they founded a number of lodges. This Scottish-Templar legend can also be found in Cagliostro's Egyptian Rite, where in the first degree it puts forward that 'one of the Templars, who took refuge in Scotland, follow the Freemasons to the number of 13, afterward 33…'[72]

The sixth degree of *Philosopher* focusses on examining the initiate if he is 'sufficiently instructed in secrets of the Chamber of Wisdom' and if so, he can move forward to discover the 'hieroglyphs', the initiate being reborn and qualified to assist the aim of Freemasonry in restoring the Golden Age.[73] The final seventh degree of the *Grand Priest of the Temple* or *Spiritual Knight* is a dramatic conclusion to the rite; the degree being filled with references of alchemy that put forward that the initiate is finally attaining the secrets of the old philosophers; the secrets of divine magic handed down from 'three pupils of Pythagoras and Zeno…'.[74] This final degree has been described by historian Robert Collis as the most profound expression of Illuminism,[75] and does indeed present a concluding spectacle that presents the candidate with the lost knowledge of the ancients. In 1782, Secret

Societies became forbidden in Russia, and although Freemasonry was not affected, Melissino appears to have retired and withdrew himself from the Order, his lodges eventually closing.

The Rite of the African Builders or Architects

This rite has obscure beginnings according to Waite; it may have been founded around 1766 and there is certainly some mystery surrounding its organisation. J.W.B. von Hymmen has been mentioned by Waite as being associated to the Rite of the African Builders or Architects, along with C.F. Köppen, who was the founder. Like the Rite of Strict Observance, the rituals were performed in Latin, and Hymmen, who was a Prussian Judge, was said by Waite to have been a member of the Strict Observance. There is some debate as to the Masonic nature of its degrees, although Waite presumes that a member had to be a Master Mason before joining. There are two different accounts presented by Waite of the actual degrees they practiced; the first of which includes the Inferior Grades of *Apprentice of Egyptian Secrets*, *Initiation into Egyptian Secrets*, *Cosmopolitan or Citizen of the World*, *Christian Philosopher*, *Alethophiles or Lover of Truth*, and High Grades of *Esquire*, *Soldier* and finally *Knight*. The second account gives the degrees as *Knight* or *Apprentice*, *Brother* or *Companion*, *Soldier* or *Master*, *Horseman* or *Knight*, *Novice*, *Aedile* or *Builder*, and finally *Tribunus* or *Knight of the Eternal Silence*.[76]

Looking at the first account of the degree system, the rite seemed to concentrate on Egyptian secrets and mysteries, giving an interesting fashionable and exotic flavour to the grades, reminding one of Cagliostro's Egyptian Rite. It certainly attracted the literati of the time and was established for the purpose of 'literary culture and intellectual studies', being an Order that appealed to the intelligentsia, and for a short time 'lodges' were operating in Worms, Cologne and Paris. However, the rite was short lived, and according to Gould writing in his *History of Freemasonry*, the rite died with the death of Köppen in 1797.[77] Despite its relatively short life, the rite has certainly attracted the attention of Masonic writers such as Gould and Waite, who seemed to find it an intriguing example of a lost rite.

Rite of Egyptian Priests

Egyptian styled Freemasonry certainly flourished during the later eighteenth century, with the aforementioned Cagliostro's Egyptian Rite and the Rite of African Builders. However there is another example with the rather obscure Rite of Egyptian Priests, which is yet another rite that explores an esoteric form of initiation with an arcane Egyptian backdrop. Nick Farrell presents a translation of this para-Masonic Rite of the Egyptian Priests, derived from a German work entitled *Crata Repoa* dated from 1770, a translation having previously been conducted by Ragon in the nineteenth century.[78] The rite contained seven Grades; the first being *of the Pastophoris or Apprentice*, the second *Neocoris*, the third grade is *The Door of Death*, the fourth is *The Battle with Shadows*, the fifth *Balahate*, the sixth is entitled *Astronomus before the Gateway of the Gods*, and the seventh and ultimate grade is *Propheta or rather Saphenath Pancah, he who knows secrets*. The seven grades from apprentice to Propheta reflect other rites of the period such as the Rite of Philalethes that provide the journey from a novice to becoming a prophet who finally has the lost knowledge of the ancients revealed to him.[79]

With an obvious Egyptian theme running through the rite, an Egyptian setting dominates the performance of the grades; the Sphinx and mummies are mentioned, and in the grade of *The Door of Death*, a room is revealed with 'various sorts of embalmed bodies and coffins.'[80] The death of Egyptian and Greek Gods such as Typhon, who is killed in the fifth grade by Orus (Horus), are also portrayed as the candidate progresses on his journey.[81] The rite is indeed a rather mysterious one, and as Farrell writes in the introduction of the work:

> *Historically its claims are bogus or unlikely but have been upheld by groups that used it as a template including the European Esoteric Freemasonic Groups*' and that the rite is a '*small, and largely forgotten work*' which '*was influential on the development of the Western Mystery Tradition. These in turn influenced the English speaking Rosicrucian Orders including the Golden Dawn, OTO, AMORC, Builders of the Adytum and Dion Fortune.*'[82]

Thus, according to Farrell, this relatively small and forgotten rite becomes significant when looking at how the occult revival of the later nineteenth century developed and how the revival was influenced by the earlier esoteric rites of the eighteenth century.

The Bavarian Illuminati

Another Society that certainly attracts attention today is the Illuminati; a

Society which was originally non-Masonic and was founded in Germany in 1776, by Adam Weishaupt. Weishaupt, a professor of canon law at Ingolstadt University, had originally devised the concept of a secret society filled with his most enlightened students. With the Owl of Minerva perched on an open book as their symbol, the Illuminati, which was designed to support the ideas of the Enlightenment, eventually worked a number of grades that expanded on Weishaupt's ideas. The idea behind the name 'Illuminati' echoed the members' fight against darkness, but originally Weishaupt was going to call the Society the 'Bee Order', and its members were called Perfectibilists; the Order striving for the improvement of human nature and society. Weishaupt joined a lodge under the Rite of Strict Observance in 1777, and after being introduced to the first three degrees of Freemasonry, decided to form his own lodge of Illuminati members, thus merging the two.

The recent work on the Bavarian Illuminati *The Secret School of Wisdom* provides an excellent presentation of the formation of the degrees and how Masonic elements were added to the Illuminati system.[83] This was done with the help of Baron Adolph von Knigge, who had become disenchanted with the Strict Observance and its elusive unknown superiors, and embraced the Illuminati wholeheartedly. Some of Knigge's ideas included a Table Lodge, and an overall Christian flavour that culminated with an idea that Hiram was actually Jesus, Freemasonry being a way of propagating his secret teachings. Knigge was also aware of the aforementioned Rite of Egyptian Priests through the exposé *Crata Repoa*, the fourth degree of which is called *The Battle of the Shadows*. This degree certainly resounds in the Minerva degree of the Illuminati, especially with the occurrence of the adept in *The Battle of the Shadows* being given a shield called 'Minerva' and then awarded a medal which reveals Minerva as an owl.[84]

The grades according to Waite, became a mixture of the political, the intellectual and the Masonic, with Waite putting forward a number of parts to their system; Part A included the Preparatory degrees of *Novice and Teacher*, *Academy of Illuminism* or *Minerva degree*, followed by *Illuminatus Minor* and the final degree of *Illuminatus Major* or *Magistrate of the Minerval Church*. Part B followed with the Intermediary degree of *Scottish Knight of Illuminism*, which appears to have been inspired by the popular fashion for the *Écossais Grades*. The progression continued with Part C, which Waite termed the Class of the Lesser Mysteries and included *Epopt* or *Priest of Illuminism*, and this priestly degree was followed by

Regent or *Principatus Illuminatus*, which Waite refers to as a more political degree. Part D is given as the final stage and was titled Class of the Greater Mysteries, which included *Magus* or *Philosopher* and finally *Man-King*. The system certainly reflected the journey from 'Novice' to 'Philosopher' that so many of the other rites conducted. The degrees may have been different, but they shared similar themes. The Illuminati of Bavaria was finally supressed by an electoral edict in 1784, and Weishaupt's vision of human perfectibility came to an end.[85] The name of the Illuminati is perhaps more widely known today for being embraced by speculative authors and conspiracy theorists as an umbrella term for a wide range of collective secret societies, but the true history of the Order is far more interesting and appealing, especially as the original ethos of the society was to bring light in the form of maintaining the ideas of the Enlightenment. There are various groups existing today that work the grades of the Bavarian Illuminati, though these are more recent revivals and have no continuity with Weishaupt's original Society.

Fessler's Rectified Rite

With so many rites being practiced during the eighteenth century, there were attempts to reform them, to retain certain elements that appealed and discard the parts that did not. Fessler's Rectified Rite was an attempt to reform the various Masonic degrees of the period, but unlike Willermoz's Rectified Scottish Rite, Fessler's Rite was a little less successful to say the least. Ignaz Aurelius Fessler was a Hungarian who took Holy Orders, becoming a novice in a monastery at the age of seventeen in 1773. He became disaffected with monastic life and in 1783 he became a Mason at Lemberg, and soon developed a desire to reform Freemasonry. Fessler was a member of the Lodge Royal York of Friendship, eventually forming a new constitution and establishing it as a Grand Lodge in 1798, also extending an educational aspect to the project by creating a Scientific Masonic Union that was dedicated to historical study of Masonic science.

The rite itself was adapted from numerous sources such as the French Rite, the Strict Observance, the Chapter of Clermont, the Swedish Rite and the Ordo Roseæ et Aureæ Crucis, Fessler seemingly putting together a balance of the Masonic, esoteric and chivalric grades. Waite thus puts forward Fessler's degree system; the first three Craft degrees followed by a Chapter of Higher Knowledge which included *the Holy of Holies*, *Justification*, *the Celebration*, *the True Light*, *the Fatherland*, and finally

Perfection. The rite was abandoned in 1800, and Fessler himself 'resigned all honours and offices' two years later, though according to Clavel's *Histoire Pittoresque de la Franc-Maçonnerie* some Prussian lodges were practicing the rite around 1840.[86]

The Rite of Perfection and the Order of the Royal Secret

We now know that the Rite of Perfection consisted of the first part of 14 degrees, while the 25 degrees of the rite (including the first three Blue Lodge degrees) were collectively known as the Order of the Royal Secret.[87] The system appears to have been compiled by French trader Estienne Morin. Morin had been involved in high grade Freemasonry since the 1740s, his trade to the West Indies allowing him to establish the Order in Jamaica and North America. Morin was helped by Henry Andrew Francken, another French national of Dutch extraction who Morin made Deputy Grand Inspector General. It was Francken that travelled to New York and established the rite there in 1767, and from there, the Order went on to be founded in South Carolina, which ultimately led to the establishment of the Scottish Rite there in 1801, the Scottish Rite becoming one of the most well-known and enduring rites that it still widely practiced today. Francken worked with Morin on the rite and wrote a number of manuscripts which gave details of the grades, what is referred to as the third of these manuscripts eventually fell into the hands of a certain Michael Alexander Gage in the north-west of England.

Michael Alexander Gage and the Francken Manuscript

Michael Alexander Gage was one of the presiding architects of the Liverpool Masonic Rebellion of 1823, the rebellion effectively relaunching the Antient Grand Lodge. The rebellion was a reaction against the ritual and administrational changes ushered in by the union of 1813, a union that had brought the Moderns and the Antients together. The issue of the Royal Arch was of much contention, the Antients practicing the ritual as a separate degree, the Moderns officially recognising the Royal Arch as the completion of the third degree. Gage was born in Kings Lynn, Norfolk, in 1788 and joined a lodge there, becoming Worshipful Mater of the lodge in 1810. He then moved to Glasgow the following year, where he also joined a lodge, finally settling in Liverpool in 1812, where he became a prominent member of an Antient lodge named Lodge No. 20.[88] Gage was a firebrand of a man; his demands for regulation change and his ensuing letter to the Grand

Master the Duke of Sussex revealed his strong passion for questioning the union, but Gage was also deeply interested in ritual, and was the owner of a rare copy of the Francken manuscript.

This Third Francken MS as it has become known, is indeed a remarkable document; Gage writes at the beginning of the document that it was 'Received from John Caird, Edinburgh - Jas. Caird, Liverpool 30th August 1815', and it was still in his possession fifty years later.[89] The manuscript gives a description of 25 degrees of the Order of the Royal Secret, the precurser to the Scottish Rite, and was certainly of interest to Gage, who kept the manuscript long after he left the rebel Grand Lodge. Gage's dream of a relaunch and expansion of the Antient Grand Lodge started to disintegrate only a few years after its conception, when internal disagreements was to see the Grand Lodge move permanently to Wigan and become more local in its outlook. This 'Wigan Grand Lodge' had a small number of lodges operating in the industrial north-west of England during the 1840s, with

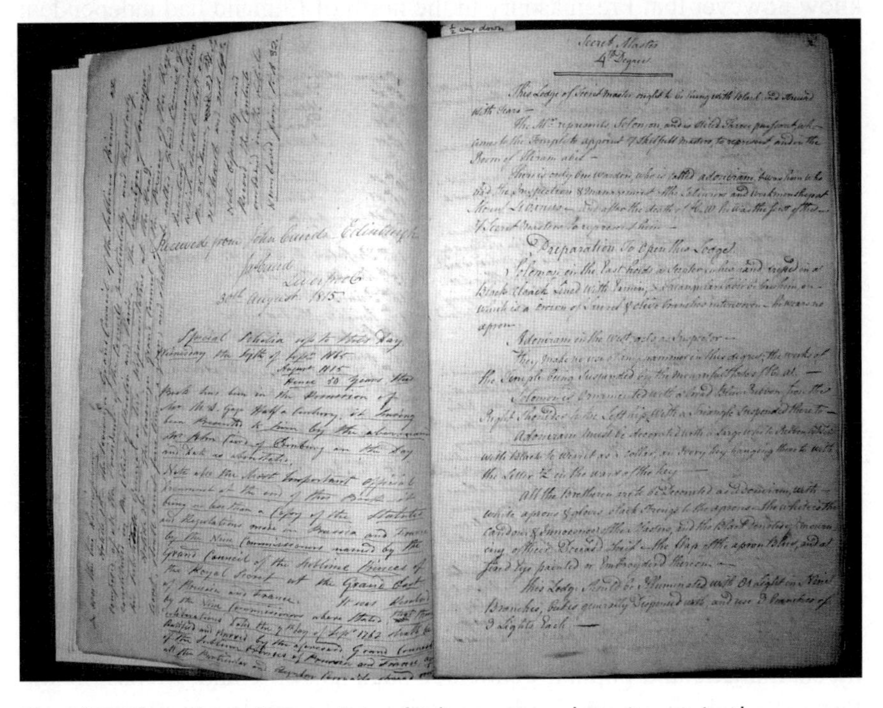
Secret Master
4th Degree

Received from John Caird Edinburgh
J Caird
Liverpool
30th August 1815

Preparation To Open this Lodge

The Third Francken Manuscript, which mentions how it was in the possession of M.A. Gage from 1815-1865.
Library and Museum of Freemasonry

two lodges operating in Wigan, one in Warrington, one in Liverpool, a lodge in Ashton-in-Makerfield and a lodge in Ashton-under-Lyne, and like the Antients, they practiced the Royal Arch as a separate degree.[90]

In his resignation letter to the Wigan Grand Lodge in 1842, Gage outlined that he had not attended a lodge for fifteen years, and he declined a request to write a pamphlet about the rebellion. It seemed that Gage had long been disenchanted by the route the rebels had taken, and was greatly concerned by the 'great irregularity in Numbering and granting of New Warrants' for the lodges, being upset at not being given the opportunity to inspect the new Warrants before they were issued.[91] So had Gage wanted another direction for the Grand Lodge? And did this direction include the practice of the 25 degrees presented on the Francken Manuscript? The fact that he still had the document in 1865, long after he had resigned and even longer since he had attended a lodge, certainly reveals a deep interest in the rite. However, we can only speculate on his ultimate grand design. We do know however that Freemasonry in the north of England had independent flourishes, such as with the York Grand Lodge, which operated at intermittent periods during the eighteenth century, and of course the aforementioned Liverpool Masonic Rebellion and the subsequent Wigan Grand Lodge. Before the union, as we shall see in a later chapter, the ritual was varied and could be diverse, and there was an old Lancashire ritual which was once practiced.

Conclusion

The majority of these rites included a similar structure; they started with the three Craft degrees, and then built on these by exploring the Scots or Scottish Master Grade, such as the Rite of Strict Observance, Rite of Philalethes and Melissino's Rite. The initiate then went on to sample Chivalric degrees until finally, like the Philalethes and Melissino Rites, a degree of Philosopher opened the way for the initiate to attain a full spiritual understanding with the discovery of the lost knowledge of the ancients. This high grade style of Freemasonry was certainly popular on the Continent, especially in France and Germany, and besides offering a further pathway for the Freemason to explore the arcane secrets on offer, they were managed by charismatic and popular gentlemen such as von Hund, Melissino and Pasqually, which would also be an attraction to gentlemen searching for pathways to investigate. The additional appeal of having access to the teachings of alchemy, magic and the Kabbalah that were offered in certain rites such as Cagliostro's Egyptian Rite and Melissino's Rite, provided an additional attractive aspect for one's search for the lost knowledge of the ancients, and attracted men (and women) to join and to socialise in the orbit of their particular charismatic leader.

Many of the men behind the lost rites discussed here were clearly misunderstood; Count Cagliostro for example will forever remain an enigmatic and confusing historical figure, his mysterious past and dramatic demise creating deliberation amongst historians. Baron von Hund will also persistently attract debate whether or not he actually met the mysterious Unknown Superiors, if he was duped by con-artists or if he really met with the Knight of the Red Feather. Others, such as Zinnendorf, clearly had ambitions of their own and became leading figures in Freemasonry.

Despite the popularity and zeal of the high grade rites that sprang up during the eighteenth century on the Continent, there was a reaction in an effort to bring Freemasonry back to the significance of the Craft degrees. This reaction to what was seen as the pretentiousness of high grade Freemasonry is best exemplified with the Grand Lodge of the Eclectic Union, which began around 1783, and according to Waite may well have still been meeting in Frankfort-on-the-Main and prior to 1914, Waite noted that there were 21 lodges under its sway with 3000 members. It seems not all Freemasons were too keen to explore new pathways.[92]

Many of these rites failed to survive after the death of their founder; Cagliostro's Rite disappeared after his death and the Rite of Strict Observance also ceased to function in its original form after the demise of von Hund. The Rite of Strict Observance however, was reformed and restructured by Willermoz, who also absorbed elements of the Rite de Elus Coens into the new structure, creating the Rectified Scottish Rite, otherwise known as Chevalier Bienfaisant de la Cité Sainte, a rite that still exists today. This rite evolved from the 1778 convent at Lyons and finally took shape after the 1782 convent of Wilhelmsbad, led by Willermoz himself, who combined the Templar themes of the Strict Observance with the religious themes of Elus Coens. Willermoz had been prominently involved in both rites, and the Rectified Scottish Rite is certainly an example of a rite that emerged from the blending of different Masonic ideas. Ideas do seem to have been shared, and certain parallels do exist between other rites, something that will be examined in the next chapter especially when examining aspects of Cagliostro's and Melissino's ritual content. The Order of the Royal Secret also transformed into the Scottish Rite in South Carolina during the early nineteenth century, the rite developing from 25 degrees to a total of 33 degrees.

In the next chapter we will examine the lost esoteric nature of certain rites; rites such as the Rite de Elus Coens, the Order of the Gold and Rosy Cross and the Egyptian themed rites that held elements of alchemy and spiritualism. Some of these rites offered a spiritual pathway that promoted ideas found in the Western Esoteric Tradition, allowing intellectuals to freely explore esoteric concepts during the age of Enlightenment.[93] Intellectuals such as Saint-Martin and Georg Forster divulged in these esoteric rites, seeing it as yet another way to search for hidden knowledge. As we shall see, a number of these rites offered a pathway to God himself; a pathway of grades that took the Master Mason on a journey of self-discovery and allowed the worthy to commune with the Divine.

Chapter 2

Les Hauts Grades Ésotérique Perdu: a pathway to God

Masonry has among its brethren Enoch and Elias.
Cagliostro's First Degree of the Egyptian Rite.[94]

For we are the Brethren of the Rosie Cross. We have the Mason Word and second sight.[95]

The kind of practice was that which endeavours to establish communication with unseen intelligence by the observances of Ceremonial Magic.[96]

As we have seen, the first three degrees and ultimately the Royal Arch were concerned with finding the lost word of God, but some of the rites that were developed on the Continent during the eighteenth century went further; the more mystical rites such as the Rite de Elus Coens and the Swedenborgian Rite contained elements of the use of magic that offered their members a way to commune with God himself. Contacting supernatural Beings or Angels was considered a very real practice in the eighteenth century, and attracted kings, members of the aristocracy and the intelligentsia of the period. As we shall see, what were, and still are, considered occult practices also attracted certain rational men of science. These occult practices were certainly not new, a well-known example of similar rituals for contacting spirits and angels being seen in the later sixteenth century with the magician John Dee and his scryer Edward Kelley. Indeed, the same practices were later attempted by Freemason Elias Ashmole in the mid-seventeenth century. There are also Biblical references of prophets such as Moses and Enoch communing with God, and some of the lost rites engaged directly with this pursuit, combining the search for lost knowledge with esoteric studies into nature and science that explored magical and alchemical practices.

John Dee and Edward Kelley; Communion with the Angels

With a blend of alchemy, scrying and summoning, John Dee and Edward Kelley made up one of the most sensational occult partnerships of all time. Dee, in some respects, could be considered an early scientist; he was an expert in navigation, he was invited to lecture on Euclid's Geometry at the University of Paris in his early twenties, and he was a mathematician. Yet, his search for lost knowledge knew no boundaries, and magic became another pathway for him to thoroughly explore; astrology, alchemy, divination, scrying and summoning were all ways in which Dee sought answers.

Dee became a special advisor to Elizabeth I, advising her in astrology and on matters of science; he chose Elizabeth's coronation date and advised on the voyages of discovery. In short, Dee was a leading expert at the Elizabethan Court and used both science and magic to search for knowledge. However, it was his partnership with Edward Kelly that he is probably best remembered, along with his studies into the Enochian language of the Angels. Dee met Kelley in 1582, and was impressed by Kelley's srying ability, employing Kelley to work for him. Kelley however had a rather chequered past, being convicted for forgery, and some modern writers and historians believe he was nothing more than a trickster and an 'occult charlatan'.[97] Dee was convinced of Kelley's talents, and what resulted of their partnership was a vivid collection of encounters with Angels and notebooks filled with their language. The partnership took them to Poland, where Dee had a meeting with the Polish King Stefan.

Dee and Kelley's partnership ended a few years after a wife swapping incident in 1587 that was, according to Kelley, ordered by the Angels. Dee returned to England two years later, leaving Kelley on the Continent, where he became an alchemist in the employ of Rudolph II. Rudolph imprisoned Kelley – probably in an attempt to stop him escaping until he had produced gold – and Kelley died after an escape attempt in late 1597/early 1598. Dee died at his home in Mortlake in 1608/1609.

Linguist David Laycock puts forward in his work *The Complete Enochian Dictionary* the suggestion that Kelley was feeding Dee's lust for knowledge, the Enochian language itself being open to interpretation, but also that the language could be a cipher of sorts – a code that has yet to be cracked. After Dee's death, his papers were passed to Freemason Elias Ashmole, and Ashmole spent a good deal of time and effort researching the difficult text. He was fascinated by Dee and Kelley's work, and tried to commune with the angels during a succession of séances from 1671 to 1676.

The legacy of Dee and Kelley's collaboration was the language of the angels, but as Laycock suggests that there is a possibility that Kelley invented the language, duping Dee, as Kelley did all the scrying work, relaying information back to Dee.[98] However, even Laycock puts forward that Kelley may have had genuine visions and the language of the angels may have been difficult to understand, leading to mistakes.[99] Was Dee the victim of an Elizabethan conman? Dee was passionate about the work and believed that lost knowledge could be gained from these conversations, Dee believing firmly in the work that Kelley did. So, was Dee a victim to a hoax or did they converse with angels?

The Esoteric Teachings of Martinez de Pasqually

Nonetheless, Dee and Kelley's system of communicating with angels was certainly similar to the work that was conducted almost two centuries later by certain members of the Rite de Elus Coens, and was certainly reminiscent of Swedenborg's mystical beliefs, the search for lost knowledge being such a dominating theme of these rites. Jean-Baptiste Willermoz received training as a member of the Rite de Elus Coens by Martinez de Pasqually himself, training that, according to Waite, took place outside the lodge and was not part of any lodge room working, but was to be practiced alone and in private.

Yarker in his *Arcane Schools* also described how Pasqually developed his rituals, the details of which were taken from a letter; 'I have been received Master Coen, in passing from the triangle to the circles', Yarker adding that Pasqually 'sought union with deity'. In seeking this union, Yarker went on to explain how Pasqually:

> *...traced the Initiatory Circles, and the Sacred Words himself; and prayed with great humility and fervour in the name of Christ. Then the super-human beings appeared in full light to bless the labours. After these had departed Martines instructed his Disciples how to obtain like results, and it was to these only to whom he gave the 7° of Rose Croix.' So according to Yarker's presentation of the 'training', it was an integral part of the final Rose Croix degree.*[100]

The training was indeed an essential part of Pasqually's teachings and between 1768 and 1772; Willermoz received instruction from Pasqually 'in occult or magical procedure'.[101] These included not eating meat, conducting the ritual three days at the beginning of either equinox – the ritual to be performed at midnight, and to wear particular clothing while being divested of metals. A circle of retreat was to be drawn in the west side of the room with 'the proper inscriptions at the proper points, with the symbols and wax tapers', with a segment of a circle drawn on the east side of the room.[102] After lighting all the tapers, the name of God was supplicated, and the names of the inscribed angels were recited, being asked 'to grant that which was desired…'[103] However, in spite of his dedication, Willermoz only reported seeing visions of colours, sparks and the feeling of goose bumps, ultimately becoming dissatisfied with the results.[104] His close friend and colleague Louis-Claude de Saint-Martin – who became known as the 'Unknown Philosopher' – believed that there could be a direct communion between man and God, and that 'we are all Christs'.[105]

Around 1770, Pasqually gave Willermoz further instructions, with the circle of retreat being located in the centre of the room, but by 1772, Pasqually left for St. Domingo, never to return and the Rite de Elus Coens came to an end. As Waite enigmatically puts forward, 'I do not doubt that Willermoz and his circle received psychic communications',[106] Willermoz and Saint-Martin's explorations for the search for lost knowledge pushing the boundaries of this world…and that of the next. As Waite reminds us 'the Ceremonial Magic of the Elect Priesthood is by no means fully available…' and there were certain invocations and descriptions that were not written down, so the little we do know gives us but a glimpse of Pasqually's occult workings.[107] We do know however that part of their doctrine featured a belief system of the Fall of Man and the restoration of man as a divine agent, being able to commune directly with God.[108] Richard Ambelain in his book *Le Martinisme* was also unclear about the exact structure of the Elus Coens rituals, but he did present correspondence by Saint-Martin that also explained similar magic rituals. These contained instructions on daily invocations, a daily work that could begin from the beginning of a new moon until the end of the first quarter, and a drawn circle marked with east, south, west and north. There was also a short ordination of the Grand Architect and a reminder of the spiritual entities that may be encountered.[109]

As we have seen, the occult revival of the later nineteenth century was ultimately fuelled by the desire for this communion with supernatural beings, be it Dee and Kelley's scrying system or the mystical high grades and teachings of the Swedenborgian Rite or Martinism, with Freemasons such as Arthur Edward Waite, John Yarker and Aleister Crowley being captivated by the search for lost knowledge.[110] Martinism became popular in the later nineteenth century and was dedicated to the teachings and philosophies of Saint-Martin and Pasqually. This recreation was conducted by Gérard Encausse, whose esoteric pseudonym was Papus, and who claimed to have several of Saint-Martin's original notebooks, something that Papus hoped would give some legitimacy to the revival. Papus is also noted as copying part of Cagliostro's Egyptian Rite from a transcription taken from an original copy.[111]

According to Papus, the book *Des Erreurs et de la Vérité* (the first book by Saint-Martin published in 1775) was due almost entirely to a 'Being' whom Papus called *La Chose*, a being also referred to as the 'Unknown Philosopher' which manifested in response to invocations, and that it was this 'being' that gave forth the work, dictating to Saint-Martin 166 *cahiers d'instruction* and giving Saint-Martin orders to assume the name of 'Unknown Philosopher'. This agent subsequently destroyed around 80 *cahiers* in 1790 to prevent them falling into the hands of Robespierre's emissaries during the turbulent years of the French Revolution. The Unknown Agent was said to have begun to manifest itself at Lyons and, according to Waite, the mysterious *La Chose* may refer to 'Pasqually's Guide in the unseen'. Waite however was doubtful of Papus' version of events and referred to him as a 'most inaccurate writer'.[112]

Waite actually put forward in his *Encyclopaedia* that the 'Unknown Philosopher or Agent' was believed to be Christ himself,[113] and according to another disciple of Pasqually's called the Abbé Fournié, Christ was actually seen, Fournié also hearing Pasqually's voice two years after Pasqually had died.[114] Papus stated that the apparitions of the 'Agent' continued at intervals up until 1796, when, as Waite put it 'the whole thing sagged out'.[115] What appears to have been happening was very similar to Dee and Kelley's scrying sessions and indeed the clairvoyant sessions of Cagliostro, with a spiritual agent giving information and orders, a séance of sorts that gave Pasqually – as a leading Magus of a magical rite – and indeed, his disciples, the access to obtain hidden knowledge.

The Mysteries of Cagliostro and the Rise of Egyptian Freemasonry

The Cagliostro ritual mentions how advice was sought from the Angel Aneal on whether a candidate had the merit and qualities to become a

Master Mason,[116] and in their work on Cagliostro, Faulks and Cooper put forward how the magician commanded 'the angels of the Divine to achieve the results according to the power of God',[117] something that Papus would have certainly recognised as being similar to the work of the Unknown Philosopher. Cagliostro claimed to be an active and powerful clairvoyant, though as the Grand Copht of his rite, he used a medium in his work called a 'dove' to consult the angels and the spirits as part of the Masonic ritual, but according to Faulks and Cooper, the Grand Copht could 'call upon the spirits of the dead'.[118]

However, in this sense, Cagliostro's clairvoyant work became entwined with his ritual, the communion with the angels and spirits being as essential a feature as the teachings of Pasqually to members of Elus Coens. Similarly in Melissino's Rite, the archangels feature in the seventh and final degree during the explanation of the *First Mystical Carpet*, especially 'the angel Metraton' who is described as 'the spirit of the Messiah, who holds sway over all the archangels, hosts and planetary spirits'. It is also stated that the 'imperfect spirits…only have the power to appear in one place, whereas an angel can be in ten places at one and the same time.' The end of the degree states how 'all human insight and wisdom, the deepest knowledge read from all chemical and philosophical texts, the most solid knowledge of ancient and modern chemistry' can be achieved 'through the sacred door of our Order', the Melissino system offering the lost knowledge of the Ancients through the guidance of the Divine.[119]

Cagliostro's Egyptian Rite has survived in written form, yet elements of the ritual remain a mystery; Cagliostro's séances for example, may be interpreted as purely symbolic in nature and may have been part of the theatre of ritual. With Cagliostro's rather mysterious background and tainted image, his claims may be seen as part of the general mania at the time for the blend of spiritualism and Masonry that attracted the social elite, thus bringing Cagliostro closer to orbit of the rich and powerful. In truth, we do not know exactly how his rituals were performed, and we know very little of the true meaning of certain words and phrases that are veiled in allegory, parts of the ritual thus being open to interpretation.

There have been a number of researchers in the past that have discussed a sexual nature to Cagliostro's Rite, which did indeed develop an erotic reputation during the later eighteenth century, with pamphlets suggesting that during the ritual, Cagliostro watched on as his wife made love to a seven foot giant. The same pamphlet, which was attributed to Cagliostro's valet, also told how a naked Cagliostro was lowered from the ceiling of the Isis Lodge while holding a snake, declaring to the female initiates of the lodge that they too must undress and partake in an orgy. With both Cagliostro and his wife being central to the ritual, and with the rite being open to both men and women of society, contemporary commentators openly discussed the sexual nature of Cagliostro's Egyptian Freemasonry; with the female initiates wearing white tunics and coloured sashes being joined by the male Masons; the sexually charged atmosphere of the evening descending into libertarian talk of equality, music, drink and an orgy of sex.[120]

Cagliostro's particular form of Freemasonry has continued to attract speculation associated with the more *libertine* lifestyles of late eighteenth century France. Another more recent theory has put forward that aside from being symbolic, a type of acacia was actually used in particular rituals to produce a psychedelic effect. Masonic researcher P.D. Newman[121] has suggested that acacia was used in Cagliostro's Egyptian Rite for this purpose, and in a transcription of the ritual, acacia is identified as the 'primal matter' that was 'created by God'. Indeed, the ritual conveys that this primal matter was known and 'enjoyed' by 'Moses, Enoch, Elias, David, Solomon, the King of Tyre, and other great ones', suggesting that acacia was an essential ritualistic ingredient. Cagliostro's Egyptian Rite as previously discussed, allowed alchemy to be explored within the Masonic framework and the ritual certainly acted as a form of teaching for alchemy, the catechism explaining how to 'bring about the marriage of the sun and the moon' and that the rite allowed for the search for the 'philosopher's stone' itself.[122]

Cagliostro's Egyptian Rite presents a lexicon of language in regards to the process of transmutation; the candidate experiences a transformation from the time he enters the Chamber of Reflection, where, for around an hour, he is allowed to view a collection of items which assists him in reflecting on the pathway ahead. Catechism was a question and answer form of ritual that created a deeper insight into the teachings of Freemasonry and in Cagliostro's ritual, it presented a glimpse into his form of Freemasonry; a Freemasonry were the candidate is introduced to an alchemical concoction of magic and possible hallucinogenic experiences. The acacia genus that may have been used is a mystery, but there are various species of acacia from the Middle Eastern region, such as *acacia laeta* or *acacia albida*, the latter genus of acacia having some medicinal properties, though it is not determined how much DMT these plants include.[123] One particular genus is *acacia nilotica* and this is common in Egypt, growing along the River Nile, the thorny plant exuding what is known as *gum arabic*, which has been used in medicines. The symbolic use of acacia within the third degree Masonic ritual represents everlasting life and is used as a plant that is placed on Hiram Abiff's grave; the shrub that came easily out of the ground after one of the brethren charged with searching for Hiram Abiff caught hold of it to assist his rising after resting, the shrub having been cut from its root. The acacia is also the traditional source of Christ's crown of thorns and was what the Ark of Covenant was constructed from.

The allusion to alchemy could, however, be of a mere symbolic nature here, the transmutation of the candidate into a Master being reflected in the change of the rough ashlar to it becoming cubicle:

> *The acacia is the primal matter and the rough ashlar is the mercurial part: and when this rough ashlar or mercurial part has been thoroughly purified, it becomes cubical.*[124]

In short, the initiate becoming the Master reflects the imperfect becoming perfect, and this in essence is what happens in Freemasonry today; a pathway to make a good man better, to commune with the Divine and to purify himself, the Mason seeking out lost knowledge and to assure that 'Omne trinum est perfectum'.

However, in the second degree of *Companion* in Cagliostro's Egyptian Rite, the candidate is offered a 'drink'. This drink is first described during the preparation of the lodge:

> *On the Worshipful Master's altar there shall be two covered crystal vases: one shall contain red liqueur, pleasant to drink, which may be wine; the other shall be filled with leaves of gold.*[125]

As the ritual gets underway, the candidate is urged to drink the 'red liqueur' to raise his spirits so he (or she) could understand the following address by the Worship Master:

> *My child, you are receiving the primal matter, understand the blindness and the dejection of your first condition. Then you did not know yourself, everything was darkness within you and without. Now that you have taken a few steps in the knowledge of yourself, learn that the Great God created before man this primal matter and that he then created man to possess it and be immortal.*

> *Man abused it and lost it, but it still exists in the hands of the Elect of God and from a single grain of this precious matter becomes a projection into infinity...*[126]

So in essence, the candidate is offered a drink that as suggested, may be wine, with the Worshipful Master indicating that he (or she) is receiving the primal matter, which has been identified as acacia. This is the crux of the theory, and is certainly an intriguing part of ritual, something similar occurring in various religious practices especially in certain South American religious groups, where *jurema wine* is consumed, which has a visual similarity to red wine but contained the root and stem bark of the *jurema preta* tree and has traces of DMT.[127] However, there was a recipe for what is termed the Elixir de Cagliostro published in a Treatise in 1871, which included possible psychoactive ingredients such as Nutmegs, Myrrh and Saffron. The Elixir de Cagliostro was, according to the Treatise, administered by the Count in a case of feeble digestion, and not in the lodge room.[128]

Apart from the Cagliostro Rite, Newman suggests that DMT may have been used in other eighteenth century rituals, namely the Melissino Rite, a rite consisting of seven degrees that, according to Newman, explored Masonry and alchemy through the altered state of perception.[129] The Melissino ritual, in a similar manner to Cagliostro's Rite, uses similar terminology, especially in relation to referring to acacia as 'matter', though Newman suggests that Melissino used fumes for his candidates to inhale from the 'burning coal' of the 'matter', instead of digesting it through drink:

> *The cubical stone is the alkaline universal-salt, which dissolves all metals and precious stones, because this salt is the mother, the origin, and the magnet of these things. The Master's Degree speaks to us of the acacia found upon Hiram's grave. This is the true matter, from which the philosophers create their treasures. It is the true light of the world, from which glorious Hiram shall rise again under the form of the Saviour. It is the burning coal of which Isaiah (in chap. 6:6-7) and Ezekiel (in chap. 10:2) speak, and which must be prepared in accordance with the secret system of the wise men of old and the philosophers.*[130]

The Biblical references given in the Melissino Rite discuss how Isaiah and Ezekiel had encounters with winged creatures or angels, who then presented the 'burning coal' to them. Isaiah had the burning coal 'that he [the winged creature] had taken from the altar with a pair of tongs' placed upon his lips, to rid Isaiah of guilt. Both Biblical references of the burning coals and the encounter with angels, suggests that the ritual could represent an allegorical communion with God, allowing the candidate to alchemically purify himself. Similar wording is used in the ritual of Fratres Lucis, with the word 'matter' being used when alchemical references are used:

> *Before receiving thee into the Order they took thee into a darkened room, this teaches thee that our Matter is found in a black state – our Earth. We also took away all the Metals thou hadst upon thee; this shows that our Matter is not found where Metals grow.*[131]

Of course, there has been certain English Freemasons who have enjoyed a life of debauchery that included over-indulgence of alcohol, laudanum and opiates; such as the poet Branwell Brontë, who was a member of the Lodge of Three Graces in Haworth, Yorkshire, and certainly Freemasons Sir Arthur Conan Doyle and Oscar Wilde wrote about the use of opium in late Victorian society.[132] Thomas De Quincey, the famous Opium Eater, though not a Mason, wrote about Freemasonry and was undoubtedly attracted to the mysteries of the Order for a time.[133] Frederick Hockley may have used opium during his scrying sessions[134] and even Crowley had his drug addictions.[135] However, there is no evidence whatsoever that these gentlemen combined their Masonic interests with any form of drug use, but their awareness of opiates reminds us how commonplace the use was amongst the gentlemen classes during the Victorian era.

So was acacia used as a source for DMT within these rites to produce a more vivid, visual and psychedelic experience? We can only speculate on the suggestive and somewhat allegorical wording of the rituals. However, certain genera of acacia from the Middle East and North Africa are known to have traces of DMT, some of the acacia plants being used in local traditional medicines, so perhaps the true nature of this 'primal matter' was known to men like Cagliostro and Melissino, and it thus gave the ritualistic experience a deeper symbolic meaning. The alchemical references are important in these rituals, especially Cagliostro's Egyptian Rite. In this ritual, the allegorical nature of transmutation is certainly symbolised by the 'primal matter', which in the first degree is required by the candidate along with a poniard, to assassinate the Master. This in itself is a ritualistic, symbolic sacrifice that represents a mercurial change; the candidate killing the Master being akin to the son killing the father. This would indeed vividly emphasise the reoccurring themes of life, death and rebirth that take place within the ritual. After the assassination, the dead body was said to be enshrouded and then purified, and after 'following out the seven philosophical transitions' the candidate can then 'bring about the marriage of the sun and the moon', which will in turn 'bring about the perfect progeny' after coming by the 'triangular stone'.[136]

Cagliostro's ritual is full of so much intertwining Masonic and alchemical allegory that it seems to be a ritual that we can easily misinterpret if care is not taken. Indeed, Carl Jung put forward in his *Psychology and Alchemy* that the *prima materia* represents 'the unknown substance that carries the projection of the autonomous psychic content', the primal matter thus having a different definition to different alchemists.[137] However, in the Cagliostro and Melissino rituals, the primal matter is indeed indicated as acacia, and if it was of a genus that contained DMT and was taken in a drink or through inhaling fumes, this matter could very well have induced a transformation of a different kind. Perhaps the effects of such primal matter resulted in an experience of Divine communion that assisted in the purification of the candidate, creating an alchemical and spiritual change as part of the journey. Cagliostro's Egyptian Rite will always fascinate us because of its rich display of imagery and its magical content. Indeed, its suggestion of communication with spirits, speculations of the use of DMT, and the alchemical allegory within the ritual, Cagliostro's Rite will always offer researchers a glimpse into a much misunderstood lost form of Freemasonry.

The Kneph by John Yarker, the main symbol for his Antient and Primitive Rite.

The Rites of Memphis-Misraïm and the Growth of the High Grades

Besides being the leading light of Martinism, Papus was also involved in Memphis-Misraïm, an Egyptian themed rite that, during the later nineteenth century, witnessed a resurgence after the fusing of the Rite of Misraïm and the Rite of Memphis, creating a rite that now has a staggering 99 degrees. The fact that this rite still exists today excludes it as being a 'lost rite', it has however changed dramatically since its amalgamation. The history of these fused rites are quite complex. Kenneth Mackenzie in his *Royal Masonic Cyclopaedia* certainly propagated the idea that the Rite of Misraïm 'arose out of Egyptian Masonry, which Cagliostro derived from an older source', Mackenzie going on to say that the rite was then successfully spread all over Italy by Lechangeur, Joly and the Bédarride brothers, eventually reaching France by 1814.[138] Hamill in his paper on Yarker in *AQC*, put forward that both the Rites of Memphis and Misraïm were established in France, the Rite of Misraïm in 1813 by the Bédarride brothers who saw it as a means of making money,[139] something that Cagliostro was also accused of doing with his Egyptian Rite. Both the Rite of Misraïm and the Rite of Memphis had an attractive Egyptian flavour and both had 90 degrees, though the Rite of Memphis increased this to 92 degrees in 1849, 93 in 1856 and 96 in 1862. Supply certainly met the demand.

The Rite of Misraïm captured the interest of Jean Baptiste Marie Ragon, who tried in vain to bring it under the sphere of the Grand Orient de France. Before renouncing the rite in 1817 however, Ragon supposedly admitted the Duke of Sussex into the Order.[140] The Rite of Memphis was apparently revived by Marconis de Negre around 1838 whose father had played an essential role in its early development in 1814. A number of lodges under the Memphis Rite were founded in France until most were shut down by the police in 1841; it was again revived in 1848 until lodges were shut down again after the coup of Napoleon III in 1851. Despite this, the rite found success in New York, with Marconis de Negre claiming sovereignty over both the Rites of Memphis and Misraïm and combined the two to create the Antient and Primitive Rite, a rite that eventually captured the interest of occultist John Yarker. The 96 degrees were thus reduced to a more manageable 33 degrees, and Yarker, who had discovered the Rite when in New York, brought it back over to England where he established a number of 'Councils'. Italian General and politician Giuseppe Garibaldi was established as Grand Hierophant of the Sovereign Sanctuary of Memphis-Misraïm between the years 1881-1882,[141] with Yarker becoming Grand

Hierophant of the Order later. Despite Yarker's work to promote the Order, in reality there were only around 300 members of the Antient and Primitive Rite in England, but even with this relatively low number, the rite survived Yarker's death in 1913.[142]

Alchemy and the Rite of the Black Eagle

Another eighteenth century rite that explored certain esoteric themes such as alchemy was the Rite of the Black Eagle. This was an obscure rite that deeply interested Arthur Edward Waite, having transcribed the system that included three grades from a French manuscript dating from the second half of the eighteenth century. He described the rite as being 'so militantly distinct from the rank and file of High Grades' that he made special note of it in his *New Encyclopaedia of Freemasonry*.[143] The 'bizarre' grades, as Waite describes them, consisted of 'figurative alchemy and a loose kind of Kabalism', the first grade describing how an eagle guarded the grave of Hiram for nine days and took flight with a branch of acacia when the body was found. The drapes in the Chapter room were black, and the black eagle itself sat between the pillars of the east; the sun being on the right and the moon on the left. Like Cagliostro's Egyptian Rite, the candidate was prepared in a Chamber of Reflection. Here, the candidate was stripped and

The tableau of the 30th Degree. *Regular Grand Lodge of Belgium*

was given a short, blood-coloured garment to wear along with slippers, being left in solitude with the doorway guarded by two brethren with drawn swords.

After being 'told to contemplate the remains of one who has perished on a false suspicion', the candidate was proved 'more unfortunate than guilty' and led into the Chapter, introduced as a worthy Mason who desires to become a Knight of the Black Eagle. The second grade appears to become more esoteric as the candidate is shown the method of advancing from west to east by 'the steps of the four elements', and Waite discusses how the Tracing Board depicts 'the grand circle' representing the Zodiac which encompasses the dead body of 'the Master Builder, whom the Great Work must bring back to life'. Alchemy is referred to by Waite as being performed by the 'Balance of Solomon', the use of which is said to be known by many of the ancient and modern philosophers.[144]

The third grade continues this theme, putting forward that the people who were shown the 'high philosophy' practiced by Solomon transmitted their knowledge into hieroglyphs and those who can interpret them will 'prolong their days'. The Knights of the Black Eagle of course possessed

Portrait of Georg Forster. It is debated if the portrait is by JHW Tischbein or Anton Graff.
http://www.payer.de/religionskritik/forster0101.gif

the key to unlock this ancient lost knowledge, though as in modern Masonry, the rite was purely symbolic in its portrayal of its themes. The third grade also produces a performance that presents the death of one of the brethren and, according to Waite, a bullock's heart is used for the candidate to stab with a poniard. As we shall see, there is similar wording to the ritual in Cagliostro's Rite; the rough ashlar represents the 'matter' in its chaotic state, the perfect ashlar however, is the same 'matter' when the perfect form of gold has been impressed thereon. The alchemical allusions are evident throughout and the symbolism as put forward by Waite compounds the vivid imagery of the cycle of death and rebirth; the restoration of life being a dominating theme with the acacia branch representing the tree of life and the pentacle which vitalises 'dead matter'.[145]

The Order of the Gold and Rosy Cross: The Search for Alchemy and Enlightenment?

The Order of the Gold and Rosy Cross, which was founded in Germany in the 1750s, was perhaps one of the most mysterious and arcane Masonic Orders that came into being. The principle founder of the Order was the alchemist Hermann Fichtuld, and indeed, alchemy was a fundamental part of the teachings of the Order. Only Master Masons were considered to be members, and the Order attracted a number of influential German Freemasons such as Georg Forster.[146] Forster was a leading intellectual figure of the Enlightenment; he had accompanied his father Johann Reinhold Forster on Captain Cook's second voyage, whose duty was to record and write a scientific report on the voyage's discoveries, which led to the publication of *A Voyage Around the World* on their return.[147] Georg Forster went on to become a Fellow of the Royal Society and worked in a number of German Universities, later embracing the French Revolution and becoming a leading light in the formation of the Mainz Republic. He died in exile in Paris in 1794. King Frederick William II of Prussia was also involved in the Order of the Rosy Cross, the king being friends with the Freemason Voltaire and surrounding himself with artists, writers, musicians as well as supporting science. Frederick William was said to have been a 'firm believer in the healing power of an elixir known to the Order'.[148]

Fratres Lucis, or Brothers of Light, were alleged to be a 'Masonic splinter of the Order of the Rosy Cross', Waite discussing the Order in his work *The Brotherhood of the Rosy Cross*.[149] Waite put forward that the Golden and Rosy Cross underwent a revolution around 1780 and the splinter Order Fratres Lucis was formed.[150] Alchemy was a dominant theme within the ritual, the first degree discussing 'the Theosophical and Divine Science and the Chemical Work', the candidate being instructed that 'the chief objects' of the Order are 'ill understood by the Freemasons', and that 'they are always seeking…Alchemy, Theosophy and Magic', their searches being in vain. The Worthy Brother is informed that he will be instructed in these matters, in order that his 'Reason may be thoroughly enlightened'.[151] The Tracing Board of the Order featured the four cardinal points, suggesting that God had bestowed the Chiefs of the Order with wisdom, and the symbol of the Hexagram was also present, being connected with the words *Aesh Mazor*, the Hexagram being a powerful geometrical symbol, sometimes referred to as the Seal of Solomon.[152] The Order thus offered the Freemason a deeper insight into the hidden mysteries of nature and science, purporting to provide light and an education on the subjects of alchemy and magic, which is not unlike the esoteric nature of other rites such as Elus Coens, Cagliostro's Egyptian Rite and the Melissino system.

The history of some of the rites from this period are indeed sketchy to say the least, and it was certainly an active time for Orders with 'Rose' in the title, which only adds to the complexity. For example, Kenneth Mackenzie mentions in his *Royal Masonic Cyclopaedia* that The Brethren of the Rose Croix of Gold was founded in 1777, the Order which Mackenzie describes as 'Alchymical and Hermetic' is said to have been mixed up with fable. He also mentions another group The Order of the Rose that was established in Berlin in 1778 by Franz Rudolph Van Grossing, which seems to have accepted both men and women and had two degrees; the first being entitled *Female Friends* and the second *Confidents*.[153]

This kind of interest in the esoteric was fashionable and certainly captivated men of the Enlightenment such as Georg Forster, and indeed it became another pathway to explore the hidden mysteries of nature and science. Alchemy was an attractive pursuit for learned gentlemen; not only for the research into transmuting metal into gold, but to find the elixir that could prolong life and cure disease. Ashmole had actively practiced alchemy in the 1650s, and a century later, some of the high degrees offered a way of learning the lost art.[154] Cagliostro's Egyptian Rite, along with Melissino's Rite and the Rite de Elus Coens, featured alchemy as an integral part of their rituals, attracting men (and in Cagliostro's case women as well) to partake in a rite that explored allegorical explanations of alchemical ideas.

In the seventh degree of the Melissino Rite for example, the 'Brethren of the Golden Rose Cross' are mentioned, and how 'in recent years a certain Rosenkreuz set himself up, who has founded a society of so-called German Rosicrucians'.[155] Chemistry is seen as Art, and the candidate is taken on a mystical journey, the degree featuring a variety of Masonic and esoteric references such as the 'Templar Cross' and 'the root of the Kabbalistic number 666'.[156] Indeed, Cagliostro's Egyptian Rite included various references to alchemy, the candidate being informed that 'Our language is

Left: Portrait of Sir Frederick Gustavus Fowke, 1st Baronet by an unknown artist c.1820. Sir Frederick can be seen wearing the pelican jewel of the Rose Croix degree. *Library and Museum of Freemasonry*

Below left and below: Rose Croix apron and sash, c.1900, revealing the enigmatic symbol of the pelican pecking her breast to feed blood to her young. *With permission from John Elkins*

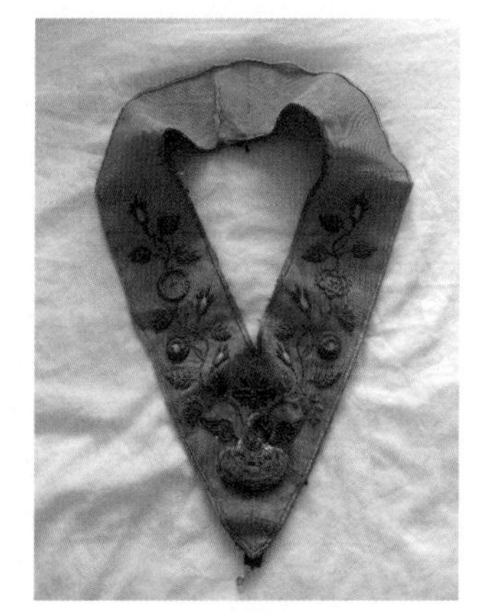

so different from that of all the writers who have written concerning the philosopher's stone', the candidate told that the 'sublime mysteries' can be revealed, in part through meditation for 'at least three hours every day' and by prayer, so that the 'arcana of nature' may be finally unveiled by 'Him'.[157] This reminds us, in a similar nature to the Rite de Elus Coens, that certain teachings outside of the lodge room were being promoted to attain a higher level of spiritual understanding. Saint-Martin for example practiced alchemy in his own private laboratory, his own personal pathway entwining with the teachings of Pasqually.

The Rose Croix: Life, Death and Rebirth

What is interesting is that some of the themes explored in these esoteric rites, such as alchemy, Rosicrucianism and the cycle of death and rebirth, filtered into part of our degree system that we still use today, something that can clearly be seen in the eighteenth degree of the Ancient and Accepted Scottish Rite; the Knight Rose Croix degree. This degree was featured in the Rite of Perfection and is included in the Francken Manuscript that was once owned by Liverpool Masonic rebel, Michael Alexander Gage. The symbol for the degree is a powerful one; a mother pelican pecks her breast to feed her own life-blood to her young, the image representing the ultimate sacrifice and also that of resurrection. The image features heavily in Christian art, and as we shall see later, the Rose Croix degree was also practiced in England during the later eighteenth century as part of the Rite of Seven Degrees in London and as part of the Baldwyn Rite in Bristol. The practice of the higher degrees also occurred in various Knights Templar Encampments in England and Wales, such as the Encampment of St. John No. 8 in the West Country which was an Encampment involved in an obscure Rite of 26 degrees,[158] and the Royal Kent Chapter in Newcastle which conferred the Rose Croix and Ne Plus Ultra degrees.[159] As Masonic historian A.C.F. Jackson observed in his work *Rose Croix*, during the early nineteenth century, various Knights Templar Encampments worked the Rose Croix and what was termed the *Ne Plus Ultra* degrees, and as we shall see when discussing the Old Lancashire Rituals in a later chapter, this certainly appears to be the case.[160]

Indeed, proof that the degree was popular at this time can be seen with the portrait of Sir Frederick Gustavus Fowke 1st Baronet, which dates to around 1820, Fowke later serving as Provincial Grand Master of Leicestershire from 1850-1856. The portrait reveals Fowke proudly displaying the pelican Rose Croix jewel and apron, and in doing so was showing off his highest degree. Another prominent English Masonic figure to have been involved in the Rose Croix degree during the early nineteenth century was Dr George Oliver. Oliver became a prominent member of the Ancient and Accepted Rite in England, helping to form the Supreme Council 33° in 1845, which was warranted by the Northern Masonic Jurisdiction in the USA.[161] As a Priest, Oliver also famously tackled the compatibility of Christianity with Freemasonry, as the Grand Master of the relatively new United Grand Lodge the Duke of Sussex sought to remove the Christian elements from the Craft.[162] Dr Robert Thomas Crucefix was also central in establishing the Ancient and Accepted Rite in England, receiving the Rose Croix and Ne Plus Ultra after joining the Cross of Christ Encampment in 1831.[163] Crucefix and Oliver served as Sovereign Grand Commander and Lieutenant Grand Commander respectively, the Supreme Council of England and Wales declaring itself established in 1846. A report in the *Freemasons' Review* that year bluntly stated the reason for the establishment of the Council 'the Haut Grades in this country have hitherto had no rallying point – no governmental discipline'.[164] Freemasons in England and Wales could now enjoy the comfort of nationally recognised progression, and the Rose Croix was thus managed by the Supreme Council.

Certainly what was termed as the 'Rosicrucians' existed in England before the year 1836, with Waite mentioning that Freemason and author Godfrey Higgins had stated that, 'He had joined neither the Templars nor the Rosicrucians'; Higgins at least acknowledging that the Rosicrucians existed within a Masonic framework at that time.[165] Papus was also said to have bestowed the Rose Croix degree on the novelist Margaret B. Peeke, a degree that, according to Waite, he sought to identify with the ultimate grade that had been practiced by Elus Coens.[166] Waite seemed convinced that the Rose Croix degree was linked directly to the older lost rites, suggesting that 'the whole arrangement of the Rose Croix Grade, its clothing, its jewel… the chambers in which it is worked, are reminiscent of the older order. The three points are in crude correspondence with the Hermetic working in Alchemy – blackness, death and finally resurrection into the red or perfect state…'[167] In essence, Waite considered the Rose Croix as being reminiscent of the esoteric grades as practiced by the likes of Hermann Fichtuld, Pasqually and Cagliostro as they sought communion with God.

Yarker, in his *Arcane Schools*, dedicates quite a number of pages to the legends and history of the Rose Croix degree, discussing the various rites that included it as a grade. Yarker emphasises the theme of resurrection in the degree, expressing that:

> *There is some analogy between the Culdee legend of the Quest for the Sangreal, and the Rose Croix Masons search for the Word. In the old Harodim-Rosy-Cross it ends in the discovery of J.M. and J., in the modern Rose Croix in the discovery of the word I.N.R.I., and has drawn upon the Catholic Miserere...*[168]

The Rose Croix degree as it is today can be seen as a Masonic version of the Passion, and with a theme of transformation, it is perhaps the most mystical and vividly Christian of the Masonic degrees. The Christian element was certainly emphasised during the early nineteenth century with the Rose Croix being conferred on a Good Friday in the Royal Kent Chapter in Newcastle.[169] The Rose Croix reflects the allegorical alchemical changes of the candidate as he purifies himself while being guided by the Arch-Angel Raphael, the degree allowing the Mason to symbolically commune with God. Thus the Rose Croix degree represents a pivotal and surviving part of the lost rites; conveying the themes of the search for lost knowledge, the resurrection and the quest for the Word itself. It can be said that as a central grade, it was used as the ultimate esoteric degree with the Mason finding his personal pathway to the Divine.

Conclusion

It is difficult to categorise these rites; for example it can be easily put forward that Cagliostro's Egyptian Rite was classed as 'Egyptian Masonry'. However, it features the Scottish Masonic legend and has obvious esoteric content, creating an appealing and fashionable rite for the period. The Rite de Elus Coens can be classed as a deep esoteric and magical rite, though it too celebrates its connection to a supposed Jacobite charter, so the rite can be seen as 'crossing over' into two categories; that of esoteric and Jacobite. Indeed, a number of the rites include obvious references to alchemy, such as Melissino's Rite, which also presents the Scottish legend. Categorising these rites has always been difficult, and we find many of the leading brethren being members of various different rites and Orders, such as Willermoz, who seemed to blend different ideas into his Rectified Rite. The esoteric nature of certain rites catered for a strong desire to examine and engage in an aspect of spiritualism and magic, and this pathway, presented in a Christian form and following a degree system that encompassed variations of the Scottish Master Grades and chivalric themes, informed the Mason within a managed set of degrees, providing an educational and philosophical journey.

The rites that were more esoteric in nature, such as the Rite de Elus Coens, certainly offered a pathway to the Divine, the arcane teachings of Pasqually being central to achieving the ultimate in celestial communion. Similarly Cagliostro's Egyptian Rite included an esoteric aspect in respect of utilizing medium work to supposedly attain the worthiness of a candidate. This again reflected the journey of the adept along a pathway of purification and spiritual union with the Divine. Indeed, in many of the rites discussed, the Rose Croix became a central degree, embodying a spiritual and Christian experience that certainly offered a pathway to God.

Some of these rites are still with us today; Memphis-Misraïm is still operating, as are many branches of Martinism. There are even groups actively meeting as Elus Coens in France and purportedly there are active members in the USA, claiming to use the original rituals of Pasqually. The problem still comes down to continuity; the majority of the rites having ceased working in the closing decades of the eighteenth century, were revived at a later stage, and even though in some cases we have the printed rituals, there are problems in fully understanding the workings of a purely written eighteenth century ritual in the modern age. The next chapter will examine how, almost a century later, a number of Freemasons began to search for the lost rites, some even using supernatural means in an effort to revive them. In doing so, they could attempt to explore the lost esoteric nature of the rituals, hoping that the secrets would lead them to the pathway to God.

Chapter 3

The Occult Revival: In Search of what was Lost

Alchemy and Masonry were early subsidiary schools of the Mysteries.
John Yarker, *Arcane Schools*.[170]

...the Sphynx holds in its colossal paws an exquisite small temple, which has Masons' marks indented into the solid walls, roof, and monolithic columns.
John Yarker, *Arcane Schools*.[171]

Therein the visible melts into the unseen...
Arthur Edward Waite, *Book of Ceremonial Magic*.[172]

With many of the rites coming to an end in the late eighteenth century, there was a noted break of continuity until many of the rites were revived in the latter half of the nineteenth and early part of the twentieth centuries in an attempt to rediscover the lost esoteric. This brave new world of the 'occult revival' witnessed a number of leading Masonic figures of the time becoming involved either in the revival or the management of various rites, occultists and 'degree mongers' such as John Yarker, Arthur Edward Waite, Papus, Kenneth Mackenzie, Samuel Liddel MacGregor Mathers and even Aleister Crowley, all deeply interested in searching for hidden knowledge. The revived rites differed to their original incarnations, either altering the degree structure as in the Rite of Memphis-Misraïm, or completely starting a new Order with little or no connection to the original rite it was influenced by, such as the Swedenborgian Rite that emerged in the US. We will now take a deeper look at some of these leading figures of what we will refer to as the occult revival.

John Yarker: Searching for Lost Rites and Rituals

John Yarker was based in Manchester in the industrial north-west of

England, and seemed to be constantly searching for hidden knowledge within the extended framework of Freemasonry, having an overwhelming fascination with further degrees and grades. He was initiated into the Lodge of Integrity No.189 in Manchester in 1854, but by 1862, he had resigned from Craft Masonry altogether. After travelling to the United States through his business, Yarker became an avid promoter and leading member of the Antient and Primitive Rite, which grew out of the Rite of Memphis-Misraïm and he thus began publishing numerous works that encompassed an eclectic mixture of subject matter which included the origins of Freemasonry, Chivalric Orders and the occult.

His work *The Arcane Schools* published in 1909 encompasses an in-depth and rather heavyweight presentation of the Mysteries of initiation, discussing various Priestly Sects and Orders from ancient civilisations to the early twentieth century; a magnum opus of sorts that also examines a history of Freemasonry, alchemy and magic. The work is a fascinating glimpse into the mind of Yarker, though the weakness of the book lies in its unquestioning approach to certain texts. Yarker was a self-educated man and as Hamill observes 'he put blind faith in ancient writers who today would be dismissed as fantasists…'[173] Despite this, the work gives an interesting look at what Yaker thought of the lost rites of the eighteenth century and supplies us with a hint of why he was so engrossed by higher degrees. Between the years 1881 and 1900, Yarker became the central force behind the publication of the journal *The Kneph*, which acted to defend the Ancient and Primitive Rite against accusations from *The Freemason* of

Symbols taken from John Yarker's publication *The Kneph*.

being irregular or clandestine. The rite was never recognised by the United Grand Lodge of England, with Yarker becoming marginalised by regular Freemasonry. The journal also promoted the Swedenborgian Rite, which Yarker was also heavily involved in, and the Ancient Order of Zuzimites, which featured William Abdullah Quilliam as a central figure.

Despite disconnecting himself from regular Craft Masonry, Yarker was still listed as a member of the Jerusalem Preceptory No.5 until 1873,[174] and Yarker later became a member of the Quatuor Coronati Lodge Corresponding Circle in 1887. He was also in contact with a number of Masons who were also fixated by higher degrees such as Arthur Edward Waite and William Quilliam, and even corresponded with Theodor Reuss and Aleister Crowley towards the end of his life in an attempt to secure the survival of the Antient and Primitive Rite.[175] Yarker was an essential mover in the occult revival of the later nineteenth century, and with his work in promoting the Swedenborgian Rite and the Antient and Primitive Rite in the US and UK, he seemed to be constantly searching for secrets and deeper mysteries within the higher degrees. His interest in the Old Lancashire Rituals were certainly part of this search, and are something that we will examine in a later chapter.

William Quilliam

Another leading figure that emerged in the Masonic world during the occult revival was William Quilliam (1856-1932), a Solicitor from Liverpool, who is now more famous for converting to Islam and founding England's first Mosque in Liverpool in 1889.[176] Quilliam was very much the Victorian polymath; he was a novelist, a poet, a campaigner for equal rights and Temperance, and he was also a Freemason. It was as a Mason that he could explore the lost esoteric; Masonry allowing him to open the hidden door to the possibilities of becoming involved in certain rites, Quilliam gaining a senior position in John Yarker's Antient and Primitive Rite, being described as Grand Examiner of the Grand Mystic Temple, 32-94° of the Province of Lancashire in 1883.[177] Quilliam was also the Most Worshipful Grand Master of the Ancient Order of Zuzimites, a somewhat exotic Order that set its ritual 1918 years before the Christian era and refers to the Egyptian God Osiris searching for Isis and the lost gem of truth. The Order met mainly in the north-west of England and there is a brief record of the Order meeting in a hotel in Southport in Lancashire for their 33rd annual sojourn in 1907.[178]

Bro. W. H. A. Quilliam, W.M.
(B.A., Persian Consul at Liverpool, Sheikh-ul-Islam of the British Isles).

Left: A photo of William Abdullah Quilliam taken from a souvenir booklet that celebrated his installation as Worshipful Master of Liverpool Lodge No. 1547 on the 13th of July 1904.
With permission from Jack Parker of the Liverpool Lodge No. 1547.

Below: A photo of the Tyler's Book of Liverpool Lodge No. 1547 showing the signature of Worshipful Master William Abdullah Quilliam, 10th August 1904. The signature of his brother Robert Ahmed Quilliam who served as Senior Deacon can be seen below.
With permission from Jack Parker of the Liverpool Lodge No. 1547.

The Liverpool Lodge, No. 1547.
OF
ANCIENT FREE AND ACCEPTED MASONS,
Masonic Hall, 22, Hope Street,
Liverpool, August 10th 1904

OFFICERS.		MEMBERS.
W. H. Abdullah Quilliam	W.M.	1
William Willis	I.P.M.	2
	D.C.	3 F. G. Toye
	P.M.	4
George Haynes	P.M.	5 H. Coleman
	P.M.	6
	S.W.	7
A. M. Morris	J.W.	8
	TREA.	9
	SEC.	10
R. A. Quilliam	S.D.	11

Quilliam's life changed drastically the following year when he was mysteriously summoned to Istanbul, and in 1909 he was struck off the Rolls, being disqualified from practicing as a Solicitor.[179] Quilliam seemed to have kept his involvement in these rites at a local level, and even though his membership of the rites was extremely prominent, he managed to stay active in regular Freemasonry, unlike Yarker who had parted ways with the United Grand Lodge of England. Quilliam was also involved in a number of Liverpool and Birkenhead Craft lodges; he was a member of the Liverpool Lodge No.1547, a member of the Royal Arch, and he was an active Mark Mason,[180] but like Arthur Edward Waite, Kenneth Mackenzie and John Yarker, Quilliam was eager to explore other Orders and Rites, searching deeper within the Masonic structure in an attempt to find lost knowledge.

Arthur Edward Waite

Of all the leading Masonic figures that emerged during the occult revival, Arthur Edward Waite was perhaps the most enthusiastic, having a keen and almost obsessive interest in the occult and in obtaining higher degrees within the Masonic framework. Waite, born in 1857, is perhaps more famous outside of Freemasonry for co-creating the influential Rider-Waite-Smith Tarot card deck, which, when published in 1909, displayed elements of Masonic symbolism embedded within the Tarot cards. Some of the cards such as the High Priestess, display obvious Masonic influence with the two pillars displayed with a 'B' and 'J' for Boaz and Jachin and with the pomegranates that decorate the background, the pomegranates featuring in the third degree. The Wheel of Fortune also appears as a possible Masonic themed card, the wheel of fortune being referred to in the working tools of the second degree, where it is said to the candidate that 'he who is placed on the lowest spoke of Fortune's wheel is equally entitled to our regard' as 'Death, the grand leveller of all human greatness' will 'reduce us to the same estate'.[181] Other symbols found within Freemasonry also occur throughout Waite's deck, such as the symbol for infinity and the pentagram, along with Egyptian imagery as displayed on The Chariot card. Waite had become a member of the Hermetic Order of the Golden Dawn in 1891, an occult society which had been founded three years earlier by Freemasons Dr William Robert Woodman, Dr William Wynn Westcott and Samuel Liddell MacGregor Mathers. His search for the deeper secrets of initiation led him to join Freemasonry in 1901, Waite becoming a rather prolific

Arthur Edward Waite in the robes of Imperator of the Fellowship of the Rosy Cross, a print from the frontispiece to volume 1 of his *New Encyclopaedia of Freemasonry*. Waite was a Freemason whose quest for lost knowledge took him onto a pathway in search for the lost Rites during a period that became known as the Occult Revival.
Library and Museum of Freemasonry

Masonic writer and historian who seemed to be in constant search for the more magical origins of the Craft, writing *A New Encyclopaedia of Freemasonry* which, when published in 1921, certainly projected Waite's esoteric leanings.[182] Of his initiation, Waite commented:

> *For myself it was a curious experience in more ways than one, and perhaps especially because it was so patent throughout that I could have told the Worshipful Master all that he was communicating to me. My Initiation was nothing therefore but a means to an end: I awaited the Grades beyond.*[183]

Indeed, Waite was anxious to explore the more mysterious and exotic further degrees which Freemasonry opened up to him, and by 1903 he had achieved acceptance into various other Masonic rites and Orders; having entered into the Societas Rosicruciana in Anglia, the Holy Royal Arch, Mark Masonry and the Knights Templar, even travelling to Scotland to receive the Early Grand Rite of 47° and then on to Geneva to receive the Rectified Rite. On his visit to Kilmarnock in Scotland to receive the Early Grand Rite of 47° in 1903, Waite seemed to be a trifle disappointed as he observed that the local brethren were not of his own social standing, stating

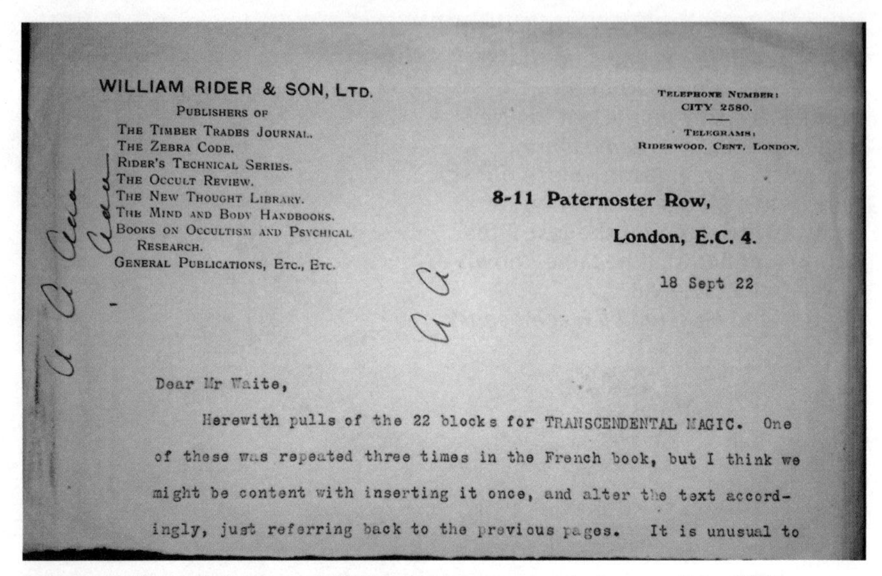
WILLIAM RIDER & SON, LTD.
PUBLISHERS OF
THE TIMBER TRADES JOURNAL.
THE ZEBRA CODE.
RIDER'S TECHNICAL SERIES.
THE OCCULT REVIEW.
THE NEW THOUGHT LIBRARY.
THE MIND AND BODY HANDBOOKS.
BOOKS ON OCCULTISM AND PSYCHICAL RESEARCH.
GENERAL PUBLICATIONS, ETC., ETC.

TELEPHONE NUMBER: CITY 2580.
TELEGRAMS: RIDERWOOD, CENT, LONDON.

8-11 Paternoster Row,
London, E.C. 4.

18 Sept 22

Dear Mr Waite,

Herewith pulls of the 22 blocks for TRANSCENDENTAL MAGIC. One of these was repeated three times in the French book, but I think we might be content with inserting it once, and alter the text accordingly, just referring back to the previous pages. It is unusual to

Letter to Waite from his publisher and notes made in pencil by Waite regarding the book *Transcendental Magic*.
Library and Museum of Freemasonry

that 'a considerable portion of them belonged to the mechanic order while one or two looked as if they were shepherds'. After the meeting and the obligatory drinks and speeches that followed, Waite wrote how 'the whole experience was incredibly squalid…'[184]

Not unfamiliar with ceremonial magic and the more darker occult practices, Waite published a variety of books on the subject; his *Book of Ceremonial Magic* published in 1913, was a repackaged work that first saw a limited run in 1898 and explored 'the complete Grimoires' and rituals, discussing what Waite termed 'true black magic' and transcendental magic. Of course Waite had already published works such as *Devil-Worship in France* and went on to publish other esoterically themed books such as *The Holy Kabbalah* in 1929. His work illustrates his wide ranging interest in magical rituals and his *Book of Ceremonial Magic* in particular certainly touches on the type of summoning work that was conducted by members of Elus Coens and indeed, Cagliostro, with Waite discussing 'Divination by the Word of Uriel', the conjuring of Demons and divination through the Mirror of Solomon. This study of various magic rituals seemed to fascinate Waite, who delved into the 'Secret of Secrets' which, he indicated, was 'the Grimoires term [for] the methods for raising and discharging spirits'.[185]

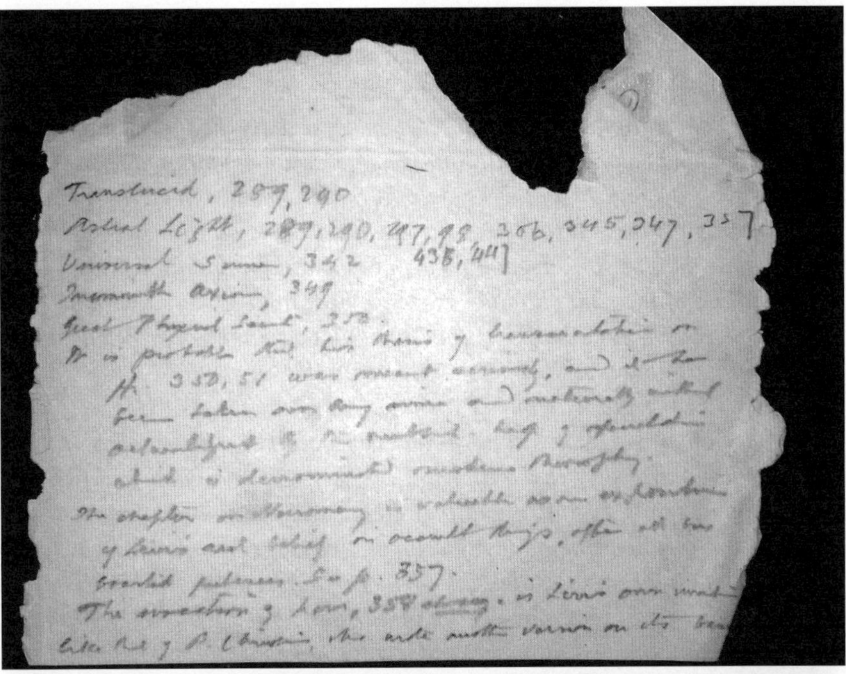

Translucid, 289, 290
Astral Light, 289, 290, 297, 98, 306, 345, 347, 357
Universal Sense, 342 438, 447
Incommunicable Axiom, 349
Great Physical Secret, 350.
It is probable that his theory of transmutation on pp. 350, 51 was meant seriously, and [illegible]
[illegible]
[illegible]
[illegible]
The chapter on Alchemy is valuable as an explanation of Levi's real belief in occult things, [illegible]
[illegible] See p. 357.
The [illegible], 358 [illegible] is Levi's own [illegible]
[illegible]

8. — PM
21 NOV 22
THREE HALFPENCE

A. E. Waite Esq.,
14, Earl's Court Square,
London. S.W. 5.

In his *Book of Ceremonial Magic*, Waite described rituals and presented symbols, and he dedicated one particular section to the invocation of Uriel, the Arch-Angel which is so familiar to the Masonic magicians:

> *To succeed in this operation, it is needful that whosoever makes the experiment shall do in all things as hereinafter enjoined. Let him choose a small chamber or cabinet which has not been frequented by impure women for at least nine days. Let such Place be well cleansed and consecrated by aspersions and fumigations. In the middle of the said chamber let there be a table covered with a white cloth; set as follows thereon—to wit, a new glass phial filled with spring water, drawn shortly before the operation; three small tapers of virgin wax mixed with human fat; a sheet of virgin parchment six inches square; a raven's quill cut ready for writing; a china ink-well filled with fresh ink; a small pan furnished with the materials for a fire. Let there be also a young boy of nine or ten years, cleanly and modestly dressed and of good behaviour, who must be placed near the table. One of the three tapers should be fixed upon a great new needle at a distance of six inches behind the phial and the two others, erected after the same manner, should stand on the right and left at the same distance. While arranging these matters, recite the following words:—*Gabamiah, Adonay, Agla, *O Lord God of Powers, do Thou assist us!*

The rather complicated ritual, as Waite put forward, led to the invocation of Uriel, the child then being asked if he can see the image of the Arch-Angel in the phial and await his communication. Uriel was said to appear in human form and was 'to bring whatsoever is desired with all tranquillity and patience, without tumult, without detriment…'[186] Waite also recalls the similarity of the 'experiments of Dr Dee', his descriptions of the ritual and results also being reflected in the clairvoyant work of Willermoz, Saint-Martin and Cagliostro.

Waite also constructed his own Order called the Fellowship of the Rosy Cross, which first met in 1915 in a hotel in London, its membership including a number of Freemasons who were active in the higher grades along with co-Masonic and Theosphical *Sorores*. The Fellowship was overtly Christian but presented an understanding of the Western Esoteric Tradition, examining alchemical and Rosicrucian ideas, and using the Kabbalistic Tree of Life as the framework for ritual progression. Though his writings were criticised in certain Masonic circles such as Quatuor Coronati Lodge, Waite gained a somewhat reverential following amongst some in the United States, being described by author J. Ray Shute as 'one of the truly great Christian mystics'. Waite was also held in high regard by American Masonic writer Joseph Fort Newton and after they met in England in 1916, Waite was awarded the rank of Past Senior Grand Warden by the Grand Lodge of Iowa.[187]

Waite was exploring all the further degrees, quenching his thirst for deeper knowledge, seeing Freemasonry as a pathway of mystical enlightenment, eventually leaving Craft Freemasonry behind as his 'activities had increased rapidly in the High Grade circles' and he 'saw more than ever the unexpressed things that lie behind the rites'.[188] He certainly saw the symbolism of Freemasonry as having the same original source as other esoteric pursuits, such as alchemy, the Kabbala and Rosicrucianism; all providing a pathway to enlightenment through the search for hidden knowledge. Waite referred to his Masonic experience by saying that:

> *...there is a Masonry which is behind Masonry and is not commonly communicated in lodges, though at the right time it is made known to the right person. But it is requisite that he should come in by the door and should pass through the preliminary grades to attain the ineffable ends.*[189]

He believed he was special enough to be accepted into the 'Masonry which is behind Masonry' – those more mysterious rituals which would only be revealed to the chosen few. He was also interested in gaining enough secret knowledge and experience to create his own rituals, Waite having plans at one stage to establish the more obscure 'Lost Rites' in England. The Hermetic Order of the Golden Dawn certainly offered a more 'magical' experience, practising ceremonial magic and using many Masonic symbols within the ritual. The Order became extremely popular and attracted writers and poets such as Waite, W.B. Yeats and Arthur Machen, though unlike many of the clubs and societies of the era, the mysterious and magical Hermetic Order of the Golden Dawn accepted women members.[190]

The Hermetic Order of the Golden Dawn

The founding of the Hermetic Order of the Golden Dawn can be traced back to 1887, when Dr William Wynn Westcott, a Freemason who was constantly delving deeper for hidden knowledge, and had previously joined Orders and rites such as the Societas Rosicruciana in Anglia (SRIA), obtained a mysterious manuscript in cipher from fellow Freemason the Rev. A.F.A. Woodford. The cipher – on translation - turned out to be a series of rituals, and Westcott asked fellow Freemason and Rosicrucian Samuel Liddell MacGregor Mathers to work on and expand them. Amongst the papers of the cipher manuscript that Westcott had received from Woodford, he had found the name of a certain Fraulien Anna Sprengal, a Rosicrucian adept from Germany, and after writing to her, Westcott was given permission to form an English version of the Golden Dawn.

The occult Order needed three Chiefs, so Westcott and Mathers brought on board fellow Freemason Dr William Robert Woodman, who was at the time the Supreme Magus of the SRIA and thus the Hermetic Order of the Golden Dawn was founded. Westcott even invited the elderly Southern Jurisdiction of the Scottish Rite leader Albert Pike to join, but he declined. Nevertheless, the Golden Dawn became exceedingly fashionable, attracting the likes of Waite and Yeats, and by 1896, there were five Temples and over three hundred members, and a Second Order was also thriving. Despite this success, there was disruption as the leaders began to fall out after Woodman's death in 1891; Westcott resigned in 1897 after his work in the magical Order conflicted with his career as Coroner and accusations of the forging the papers which had led to the founding of the society by Mathers followed.[191]

The Societas Rosicruciana in Anglia: Kenneth Mackenzie & the Séances of Frederick Bligh Bond

The Societas Rosicruciana in Anglia was formed around 1867 by Robert Wentworth Little, the society embracing Christian and esoteric elements. The SRIA attracted passionate esoteric enthusiasts such as Kenneth Mackenzie (1833-1886), Mackenzie being an occultist who felt that Craft Masonry held little appeal. Thus he left Craft Freemasonry far behind as he began to explore the high grades and journey through the lost rites, becoming involved in Yarker's Ancient and Primitive Rite and the Swedenborgian Rite. Mackenzie became an ardent writer, his *Royal Masonic Cyclopaedia* revealing his keen interest in what John Hamill termed 'the shadowy borderland between the more exotic high degrees of Freemasonry and occultism'. He had met Eliphas Lévi in Paris in 1861, and besides being a member of the SRIA, he was aware of other mysterious Orders such as the Hermetic Order of Egypt. He told Yarker in 1872 of how he had organised and developed the ritual for the Order of Ishmael, and he had joined the Royal Oriental Order of Sikha and the Sat B'hai, an Order created by an Indian Army Officer Captain J.H. Lawrence-Archer. This was not enough for Mackenzie; his search continued when he joined the Swedenborgian Rite and became its Supreme Grand Secretary, being for a time a close associate of Yarker, having joined his Antient and Primitive Rite in 1874.[192] Seemingly seduced by any rite or Order that came his way, Mackenzie, like Yarker and Waite, embraced many different exotic rites and degrees away from the confines of Craft Freemasonry as he continued to search for a deeper meaning within the ever growing Masonic framework.

Another Freemason and celebrated psychic researcher who, like Kenneth Mackenzie and Arthur Edward Waite, had also become involved in the SRIA, was Frederick Bligh Bond, an architect and a keen student of the occult. Bligh Bond knew the author and Freemason Sir Arthur Conan Doyle and they shared similar interests in psychic research, Bligh Bond having used psychic mediums to assist him in his famed excavation of Glastonbury Abbey in Somerset, which, according to Bligh Bond, led to the discovery of the Abbey being built with sacred geometry. Bond asserted that his mediums received information from dead monks, which assisted him in discovering archaeological remains of the Abbey. This rather unorthodox approach to his archaeological work eventually led him to be dismissed from the site by his employers, the Church of England. Bond went on to write about the Geometric cubit as a basis for proportion in the plans of medieval buildings and published his account of the Abbey excavation in his celebrated work *The Gate of Remembrance* in 1918.[193] His attempts at communicating with spirits certainly remind one of the mystical teachings of Pasqually for the leading members of Elus Coens.

Conan Doyle had embraced psychic research after the death of his wife and several other close family members, and until his own death in 1930, he passionately supported spiritualism and constantly sought proof of life after death, a curiosity which can be somewhat paralleled with writer and Freemason Mark Twain's interest in parapsychology in the USA. Conan Doyle's 1926 work *The History of Spiritualism* also lent his support to séances conducted by various psychics at the time and their supposed spiritual materialisations, and the theme of the séance also filtered through to his fiction, such as *The Land of Mist*.[194] For Bligh Bond and Conan Coyle, séances were an opportunity to glance into an otherworldly window, where, for a brief period, the living could meet the dead and long lost knowledge could be sought.

The Séances of Frederick Hockley & Francis George Irwin

The Societas Rosicruciana in Anglia included a number of other leading esoteric Masons who became involved in séances, in particular scrying, in an attempt to commune with spiritual beings, Freemasons such as Frederick Hockley and F.G. Irwin, both being deeply interested in the occult. Like Conan Doyle much later, it was after the death of his wife that Hockley became profoundly involved in spiritualism, becoming close to Kenneth Mackenzie, who also shared a similar passion for the occult. Hockley's scrying technique used crystals and mirrors, and like the techniques used by Willermoz and Saint-Martin in the previous century, Hockley's spiritual work took place outside of the lodge room, though his work was common knowledge amongst his close Masonic colleagues. Like Dee, Hockley thought of himself as not being powerful enough to see Beings in his crystal or magic mirror, so he used young girls to scry for him, who he termed as *speculatrix* (Latin for female watcher). This particular practice of using children or young adults for divination purposes was an ancient occult tradition that can be traced to the Egyptians and the Greeks, and was also mentioned by Waite in his *Book of Ceremonial Magic*. Like Saint-Martin before him, Hockley was said to have had success with his work, and through communication with the 'Crowned Angel', a manuscript was written called *Metaphysical and Spiritual Philosophy; or the connection with and influence over material bodies by Spirits*, but also similarly to Saint-Martin, only a few of his notes survived after Hockley's death in 1885. Hockley also attempted to delve into alchemy, asking questions when scrying to find the lost secrets of the 'Ancient Alchemists'.[195]

The parts of his notebooks that survive, outline his magical technique; the mirror or crystal was consecrated and protected by prayers, Hockley and his scryer using them only in the service of God, Hockley also invoking the name of Christ three times to summon the particular spirit guide that was needed for the task. After writing the given message down in his notebook that was conveyed from the spirit guide to his scryer, the name of Christ was again given, with a closing prayer of thanks to end the session. Despite such thorough protection, evil spirits did get through, and one incident was recorded by Hockley, and later published in the *Spiritualist* on 2 July 1880, which outlined his encounter with 'a spirit more like an animal than even a distorted human figure' that grew out of a bottle, with horns and a tail, and in a Faust-like scenario, the creature asked Hockley that he could test its power by naming anything he desired in return for obedience. After Hockley refused, the creature disappeared.[196]

The ritual that Hockley used was similar to the descriptions we were given of Pasqually's teachings and also have a similarity to Dee and Kelley's work:

> *The Invocant must in order to carry out his work have a small room in a retired part of the house such as an Attic or a low Kitchen might be preferred, made clean and neat having no sumptuous ornaments to divide or distract his attention, also free from the hurry of business and from the prying and curious intruder. The floor must be perfectly clean and even so as to receive the lines of the Circle and the characters to be traced therein. The Circle may then be drawn seven feet in diameter and the Holy Names and Characters written therein according to the following model with Consecrated Chalk or Charcoal. Should the operator not have a pair of compasses of sufficient radius to trace the lines of the Circle, he may use a piece of twine attached to a pin as a centre, and the other end to the Chalk or Charcoal. The Invocant may if he choose in the absence of the above mentioned articles, sprinkle the floor with fine sand and then draw the Circle &c. with the Magic Sword, but the first mentioned method is by far the best, and being the most durable may be so carefully used as to serve in several Operations. The room when not in use must be locked up. The Invocant must be reminded that every operation belonging to the Art must be made during the Moon's Increase.*[197]

We can thank F.G. Irwin for transcribing Hockley's surviving notebooks, Irwin going on to attempt scrying work himself. Francis George Irwin, born in 1828, was an army Captain who had gained the admiration of a number of respected Freemasons; he had met R.F. Gould and Charles Warren in Gibraltar while in the Army in the 1850s, Gould recalling that Warren had respect for Irwin both as a Freemason and a soldier. Irwin was also very much admired by Waite, who described him as 'a zealous and an amiable Mason with a passion for rites and an ambition to add to their number'. Irwin was made a Mason in Gibraltar Lodge No. 325 (Irish Constitution), and in 1866 he moved to Bristol where he delved deeper into the higher degrees of Masonry, of which, according to Gould '…there was scarcely a degree in existence, if within his range, that he did not become a member of'. Indeed, Gould went on to mention how in later life, Irwin became a somewhat passionate student of the French and German languages so he could research and translate Masonic texts.[198]

It was Irwin that introduced Hockley to the SRIA, Hockley also being an active and well respected Freemason; Hockley was initiated into British Lodge No.8 in 1864, he joined the Emulation Lodge of Improvement, became a Grand Steward, and joined the Royal Arch.[199] One particular revived rite he became involved with was *Fratres Lucis*, a rite also known as the Order of the Swastika, which Irwin had reconstructed after he had allegedly used scrying to summon the spirit of Cagliostro in 1873.[200] Notebooks in Irwin's hand describe how he contacted Cagliostro through a crystal, Cagliostro describing word-for-word the introduction to the Fratres Lucis ceremony.[201]

This revived Fratres Lucis rite soon attracted the attention of other eager seekers of lost rites, such as the aforementioned Kenneth Mackenzie and Benjamin Cox. Cox was a typical middle-class Victorian occult revivalist; a Chief Accountant from Western-super-Mare who was an avid collector of Masonic degrees, Cox also being the Grand Chancellor of the mysterious Royal Order of Knights of Eri and Red Branch of Knights of Ulster.[202] Cox corresponded frequently with Irwin and one particular lost ritual they discussed was the Ritual of the Knight of the Hermetic Cross, which Irwin was translating, possibly from the French, with Cox offering to make a copy. Cox, like Hockley and Irwin, also used a crystal in an earnest attempt to research for the deeper mysteries of occult science.[203]

In 1874, Irwin had hinted to Cox that he may be allowed to join the Order of the Swastika, leading Cox to write to Irwin, who, unable to conceal his joy at the prospect of becoming a member of such a select Order, stated that '…the one desire of my heart is to become a member of some Order wherein I may learn the mysteries of nature and truth so that I may not only benefit myself but that of my fellow men'. Cox did indeed become a member of the Order of the Swastika, otherwise known as Fratres Lucis, joining Hockley and Irwin in studying the occult arts of 'Natural Magic – Mesmerism – The Science of Death and of Life – Immortality – The Cabala – Alchemy – Necromancy – Astrology – and Magic in all its branches'.[204]

In a letter from Cox, it was indicated that Irwin even went to Paris where he apparently met members of the once lost Fratres Lucis, which is peculiar since the Order supposedly came to Irwin's attention through his 'contact' with Cagliostro. Indeed, in the notes written by Irwin concerning the Fratres Lucis ritual, the traditional history of the Order is revealed:

> *In Florence there now exists, and has existed for a great number of years a body of men who possess some of the most extraordinary secrets, that ever man has known. Cagliostro learned from them some of the most wonderful secrets in Magic and Chymistry, they converse with those who have crossed the river.*
>
> *The Members of this society are bound by a solemn oath to meet once a year, whether they are living or have passed the boundary. They are ruled by an officer, styled Supreme and Sublime Magus... The brethren take Hebrew names. There are branches of the order in Rome, Paris and Vienna. Vaughan, Fludd, Count St. Germain, Count Cagliostro, Mesmer, Swedenborg and Martinez de Pasquales were members of the order as also Schussler.*
>
> *They have made animal magnetism their chief study and have carried it nearly to perfection. It was through being a member of this society that Mesmer practised his healing power and founded his Mesmeric Lodge on the principles of the Order.*
>
> *Swedenborg derived his Rite from the same source, and from it Count Cagliostro derived the knowledge that enabled him to found the Egyptian Order; those three Rites represent three of the four grades into which this society is divided.*[205]

In short, Irwin had tidily tied together a number of lost rites and had placed their charismatic founders together in a society that met in both life and in death, and through 'contacting' Cagliostro through his crystal, Irwin had written down what Masonic historian Ellic Howe terms merely as notes for his scheme for a secret society of occultists. Indeed, the Fratres Lucis that Irwin constructed has nothing to do with the previously discussed eighteenth century Order of the same name.

So, was Irwin – a Captain in her Majesties army and a leading well respected Freemason - to be believed in his claims of contacting Cagliostro? Or was he merely misled in his belief that he did so? Mackenzie certainly believed he was in contact with the late great Cagliostro, so much so that he asked Irwin if he would authenticate details regarding an article Mackenzie was writing on Joseph Balsamo.[206] It was indeed a particularly profound way of reviving a lost rite, but it is certainly a significant moment of the occult revival with spiritualism being used by some prominent Freemasons as a means of gaining lost, hidden knowledge.

Aleister Crowley, Theodor Reuss and the Sex-Magick of the Ordo Templi Orientis

As we have seen, interest in occult philosophy captivated not only the literati of the Victorian era, best exemplified with Yeats and Conan Doyle, but also enthralled the prosperous and educated classes who wished to explore the mystical esoteric belief systems. Freemasonry and indeed, the lost rites of the previous century, were seen as a gateway that would lead to the hidden knowledge of the old magicians such as Cagliostro and Pasqually. An example of this is how Freemasonry stirred an interest in the occultist Aleister Crowley, who, in the closing years of the nineteenth century, became involved in the Hermetic Order of the Golden Dawn, joining in 1898, and from there went on to sample the hidden mysteries of Freemasonry after joining an irregular 'Scottish Rite' lodge in Mexico and the irregular Anglo-Saxon Lodge No.343 in Paris. Crowley, who believed his previous incarnations to have been Count Cagliostro and Eliphas Lévi,[207]

The seal of Eliphas Lévi taken from *Dogme et ritual de la Haute Magie*, (Paris, 1861). . *Library and Museum of Freemasonry*

later accepted an invite from Theodor Reuss to join the *Ordo Templi Orientis* (OTO), which like the Golden Dawn, admitted both men and women and had a certain Masonic influence within the ritual.

Crowley's closeness to Mathers added to growing tensions within the Golden Dawn, and it soon splintered into different groups, with Arthur Edward Waite becoming involved in the leadership of one particular faction.[208] Waite, like Crowley and other occult revivalists, were also heavily influenced by French magician Eliphas Lévi (1810-1875), who wrote numerous works on the occult, taking part in evocations, designing Tarot cards and becoming a leading authority on the concept of ritual magic. Lévi had read the works of Saint-Martin and Swedenborg, and his teachings in turn became an influence on the development of the Hermetic Order of the Golden Dawn, and certainly informed on revivalists such as Papus, also inspiring Waite's first venture into occultism; Waite writing an anthology of the works of Lévi in 1886.[209]

The lost rites of the eighteenth century certainly captured the imagination of Theodor Reuss, an Anglo-German who was seduced by the high grades as he established rite after rite in Germany. Reuss, like many of the 'Fringe Masons' and 'Degree Seekers' that are discussed here, has divided the views of many a Masonic historian over the years. For example, John Hamill described him as a 'masonic fraudster',[210] while Ellic Howe wrote he was 'perhaps this century's most fascinating pseudo-Masonic adventurer'.[211] In this respect, Reuss, and indeed the likes of Yarker and Waite, seem to reflect the divided opinions that were also made on their eighteenth century counterparts such as Cagliostro and von Hund.

After becoming a member of a London-based lodge for a short time, Reuss had attempted to revive Adam Weishaupt's Bavarian Illuminati in 1880, and after becoming friends with William Wynn Westcott, he was given a charter to establish the Swedenborgian Rite in 1901 and to set up a High Council in Germania of the Societas Rosicruciana in Anglia in 1902. Reuss contacted leading Occultists such as Papus, who provided him with a charter to establish a Martinist Order in Germany in 1901, Reuss also being in contact with John Yarker, which led him to establish the Rite of Memphis-Misraïm in Germany. However, it was in his role in founding the Ordo Templi Orientis that Reuss would perhaps be best remembered, Reuss establishing the Order with industrialist Carl Kellner, the Order developing between 1895 and 1906 and incorporating a hedonistic mix of sex-magick and Freemasonry.

On Kellner's death in 1905, Reuss took over the reins of the new Order, and on meeting Aleister Crowley in 1910, Crowley was admitted to the first three degrees and was placed in charge of the OTO in Britain and Ireland, Crowley eventually succeeding Reuss as leader of the Order after Reuss' death in 1923. The original degree structure was in fact quite similar to Freemasonry, with the system featuring *Entered Apprentice*, *Fellow Craft*, *Master Mason*, and another degree entitled the *Holy Royal Arch of Enoch*, though Crowley rewrote part of the rituals, integrating Thelema and the Gnostic Mass into the OTO system. Sex Magick is still an integral part of the present OTO structure, and since his death in 1947, Crowley has become revered by the Order.

Conclusion

The search for the lost esoteric dominated this occult revival of the late nineteenth century, with Freemasons such as Hockley, Irwin, Conan Doyle and Bligh Bond using spiritualism, akin to the rituals used by Pasqually, Willermoz, Saint-Martin and Cagliostro a century earlier, attempting to contact supernatural Beings. Masons such as Mackenzie, Yarker and Quilliam, not being content with Craft Freemasonry, explored various revived or reconstructed rites such as the Swedenborgian Rite or the Antient and Primitive Rite, delving deeper into higher degrees. These Freemasons had a thirst for lost knowledge and held a strong desire to rediscover the lost esoteric nature of the lost rites of the eighteenth century; be it Papus who claimed to have some original notes of Saint-Martin to give an authentic aspect to Martinism, or Irwin who supposedly contacted Cagliostro through scrying to obtain details of Fratres Lucis. The search for lost knowledge was certainly the driving force behind men such as Waite, who made a career out of the study of the long lost rites of the eighteenth century in a quest to discover their hidden secrets.

In the next chapter we will examine a particular collection of rituals that were used in Lancashire before the union of 1813, a seismic Masonic event that forever changed the practice of Freemasonry in England and Wales. These particular rituals captured the interest of John Yarker and Francis George Irwin, and they supply a glimpse of English Masonry before the union; an eclectic concoction of Christian references and Biblical imagery, combined with hints of older lost rituals and early catechisms.

Part II

Lost English Rituals, Symbols and Workings

Chapter 4

The Old Lancashire Rituals

...and your immediate decisive Answere to the following Question agitated amongst us, is desired, if a Man who is an Ancient Mason in the Three first degrees regularly pass'd the Chair made A.M. and S.K.T. but sitting under a Modern Warrant may be Accepted in our R.E., your Speedy Answer to this will much oblige...
A Letter from the Royal Encampment of Knights Templar in Manchester, Lancashire, to the York Grand Lodge, 1786.[212]

...in 1816, a particular method of opening and closing a lodge in the three Degrees, and of Initiating, Passing, and Raising was accepted and approved by the Grand Lodge, representing the whole of the English Fraternity.
Henry Sadler's Illustrated History of the Emulation Lodge of Improvement, 1904.[213]

And furthermore be it know that they have therein introduced a Law for the purpose of enforcing obedience to what is styled by them, the established mode of working, this new system has been opposed and rejected by an imperative Masonic Duty, because it is not 'according to the genuine Landmarks, Laws and Traditions of the Craft' as guaranteed by the third Article of the aforesaid Union, but on the contrary, it is a compound of Ancient and Modern Masonry filled up with new matter and ceremonies, to accommodate and reconcile the jarring interests and contentions of those Members who composed the Lodge of Reconciliation...
The Magna Charta of Masonic Freedom, Michael Alexander Gage, 1823.[214]

John Yarker's Masonic work, though criticised by certain writers today, has left us with a tantalising view of a Victorian Mason who entered the hidden door of the high degrees and found himself wanting more. Indeed, he never stopped searching and writing, his magnum opus *The Arcane Schools* being published a few years before his death. Yarker was absorbed by the origins of Freemasonry, and seemed to have a fascination with the York Grand

163

the Royal Order of Scotland, which gives to Masonry an entirely Christian Character. 2nd. The Lectures of the Swedenborgian Rite which assigns an Astronomical derivation of immense antiquity to Masonic Legend.

But reverting to the value of the Craft Lectures of last century, as given in this book, I cannot help saying that I consider them in many respects superior to those now in use, which are the revision of 1813 upon the union of the two Grand Lodges meeting in London. At the latter date all Christian allusions were struck out, whilst carefully retaining old Jewish Legends which have probably no basis in literal fact, and old world details opposed to Scientific fact.

Masonry, as I conceive it, is intended to form a bond of union amongst all peoples; not to make all the world Jews. And as in ancient times, we are told, Masons were charged to be of the religion of the Country where they found employment; so a perfect System of Lectures would draw its illustrations from the Truths of the old Wisdom, found in the Vedas, Avesta, Book of the Dead, and the Bible, whilst conducting by safe and implicit steps to Christian ethics.

Jno Yarker P.M. &c.

Withington,
Nr. Manchester, Nov. 3rd 1888.

1888 copy of the rituals.
Library and Museum of Freemasonry

Lodge in particular. He was a member of the Jerusalem Preceptory No.5 which met in his home town of Manchester, a Knights Templar Encampment that had originally been constituted under York in 1786. This membership and his research into older workings of higher grades that were practiced by the Preceptory, may have led him to a lodge in Warrington, an industrial town situated about fifteen miles to the west of Manchester, where he found and copied the old York Warrant for his Preceptory. At the same time he came across a curious form of catechism that had been used by a Craft lodge before the union of 1813, and Yarker subsequently copied the strange lectures in a notebook, later adding a number of old disused Knights Templar grades. Yarker called them the *Old Lancashire Rituals*.

There are four known surviving copies of the *Old Lancashire Rituals*; the first copy was transcribed by Freemason Henry White in 1863, which is kept at the Warrington Masonic Museum.[215] The second copy was transcribed by John Yarker in 1865 and is now kept at the library of the Grand Lodge of Iowa (the Grand Lodge of Iowa purchased a part of Yarker's library upon his death),[216] the other two copies are held at the library and museum of the United Grand Lodge of England, one copied by Francis George Irwin and another re-copied by Yarker in 1888.[217] The copy discussed here is the 1865 copy from the Grand Lodge of Iowa, who kindly sent a pdf version of the notebook, which includes what is termed as the Craft Lectures from pages 1 to 115. The first piece of Yarker's writing explains how the 'Rituals' were copied from an old MS book with clasps, the watermark of the paper indicating 'Durham & co. 1799' and mentioning the name 'John Smith'. The writing tells us that the book once belonged to the Lodge of St John which met in Manchester. This lodge then moved to Warrington, its members joining with the Lodge of Lights in 1830. This original written copy is currently missing.

The Lodge of St John No.322

This lodge was founded on 2 June 1769, at the Woolpack in Manchester; a Modern lodge, some of whose members seemed to have had a connection with the Knights Templar Jerusalem Encampment that was founded by John Hassall under the Grand Lodge of All England held at York in 1786.[218] Certainly one of the founders of the Encampment, a certain merchant named John Hardman, had been a member of the Lodge of St John beforehand, and for the original York Warrant of the Encampment to find its way to Warrington via the lodge, there must have been a continued connection.[219]

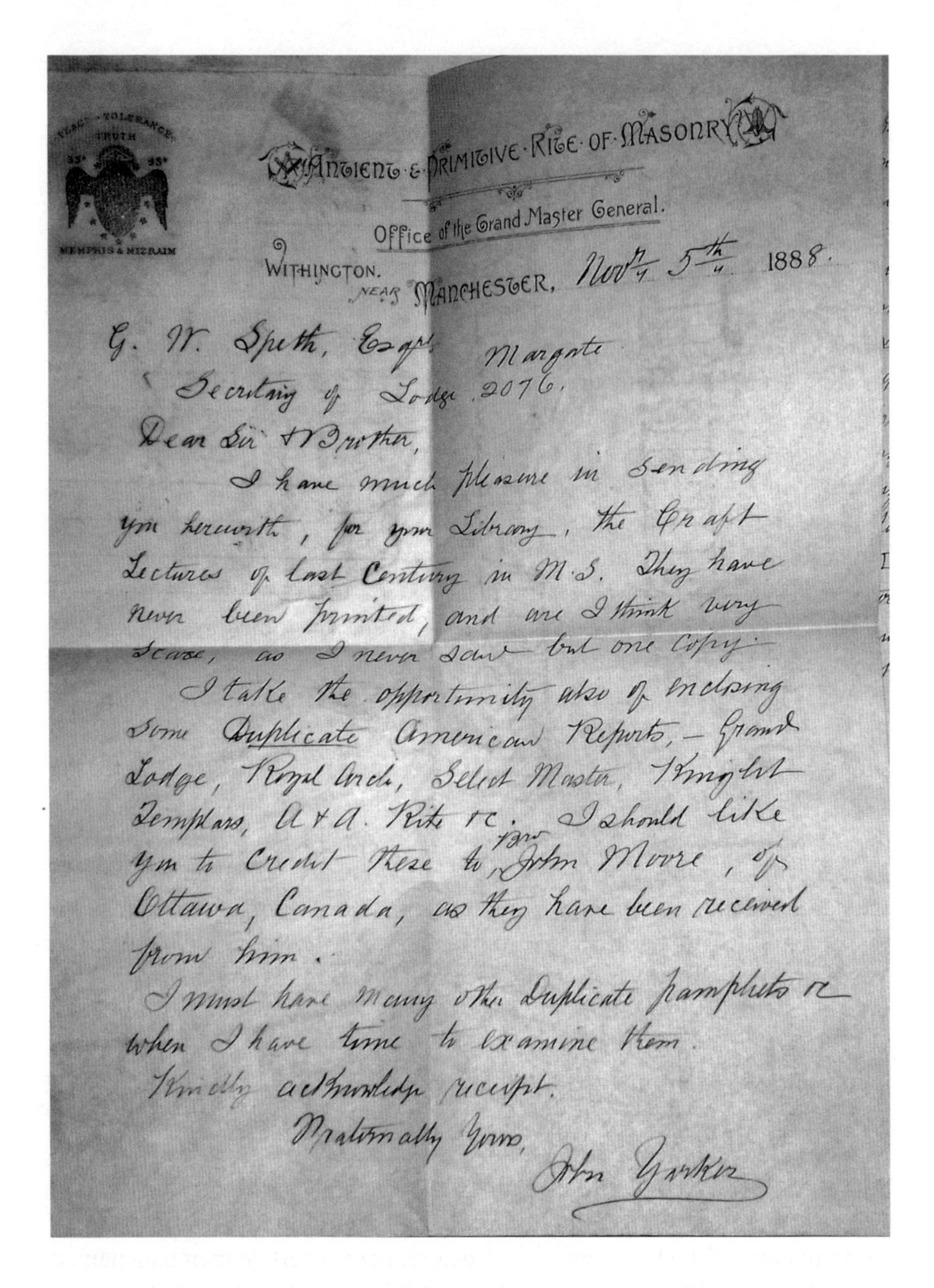

PEACE · TOLERANCE · TRUTH
33° 95°
MEMPHIS & MIZRAIM

Ancient & Primitive Rite of Masonry

Office of the Grand Master General.

Withington, near Manchester, Nov 5th 1888.

G. W. Speth, Esqr. Margate
Secretary of Lodge 2076.

Dear Sir & Brother,

I have much pleasure in sending you herewith, for your Library, the Craft Lectures of last Century in M.S. They have never been printed, and are I think very scarce, as I never saw but one copy.

I take the opportunity also of enclosing some Duplicate American Reports, – Grand Lodge, Royal Arch, Select Master, Knight Templars, A & A. Rite &c. I should like you to credit these to Bro John Moore, of Ottawa, Canada, as they have been received from him.

I must have many other Duplicate pamphlets &c when I have time to examine them.

Kindly acknowledge receipt.

Fraternally Yours,

John Yarker

The covering letter to G.W. Speth on Yarker's Ancient and Primitive Rite headed paper regarding the 1888 copy of the 'Lancashire Rituals'.
Library and Museum of Freemasonry

The Encampment broke away from York in 1795 after the demise of the Grand Lodge, and subsequently gained a Warrant under the Dunckerley Grand Lodge.

In the October of 1817 however, the Lodge of St John moved itself to Warrington and, in 1830, due to declining numbers, the lodge merged with the Lodge of Lights; six brethren joining between March-June that year, including John Smith who was a Past Master of the Lodge of St John and was most probably the John Smith mentioned on the opening page of the 'ritual' book. These joining members integrated well with the Lodge of Lights; John Smith served as Worshipful Master in 1832, another joining member Joseph Stubbs served as Worshipful Master in 1836, and another, Thomas Eskrigge served as Senior Warden in 1832. However, in 1834, the Warrant was sold to form a lodge in St Helens, and in 1845, this particular Lodge of St John moved to Bury, where it still meets today as No.191. The furniture of the original Lodge of St John was sold to the Love and Harmony Lodge No.852 in Winsford, a lodge which closed in 1851.[220] The 'ritual' book and the Warrant of the Jerusalem Encampment however, remained in the hands of the Lodge of Lights.

The Lodge of Lights (now No.148)

This lodge was warranted as a Modern lodge on 8 November 1765, and has met at Warrington ever since. There is no mention of the ritual book in their surviving minute books and there is no present tradition within the lodge of using any particular older or different ritual or lectures. Indeed, the lodge today uses a version of Emulation ritual with a few subtle differences in wording and perambulation, not unlike many lodges throughout England and Wales, and this form of ritual is the one that has been worked within living memory.[221] There have been instances within certain lodges that mention activity over ritual change in their minute books after the union, for example, the York 'Union' Lodge in 1822, mentions how no one knew the new system as they had not seen it demonstrated,[222] and the Lodge of Probity in Halifax, Yorkshire, sent a number of its brethren to learn the new working, which on their return, they assisted other lodges in Yorkshire to learn.[223] The Lodge of Lights has only recently been made aware of the 1865 Yarker copy of the ritual book and of the Henry White copy which is now on display at the Warrington Masonic Museum, and there is no mention of the original book since it was copied by Yarker.

Copyist's Preface.

The following interesting system of Lectures is apparently the version of the Sect called "Ancient", or York Masons.

The original from which they were taken in 1865 formerly belonged to Lodge "St. John" of Manchester which removed to Warrington and afterwards united with the "Lodge of Lights," and was found by Bro. H. B. White amongst the ancient properties of that Lodge. The water-mark of the paper was "DURHAM & Co. 1799," and formed a small thick book with clasps; the caligraphy being of a very superior description. The title page bore the name "John Smith" in pencil.

It may be here observed that the mention of Sir Peter Parker, Earl Moira, and H.R.H. George Prince of Wales in Part II. — Section III - must not be taken as a proof of date as the Preceptor would introduce such masonic names as were distinguished at the time when he wrote or lectured

Recopied in October 1888

John Yarker, P.M. R

Withington,
W. Manchester,

The opening description of the original Yarker copy dated 1865, showing the signature of John Yarker.
Library and Museum of Freemasonry

The 1865 Yarker Copy

The 1865 Yarker copy of the *Old Lancashire Rituals* informs us on the opening page that Yarker had been in touch with a Past Master of the Lodge of Lights, the aforementioned Worshipful Brother Henry Brown White; a Warrington based Solicitor who had joined the lodge as a joining member from Lodge No.389 on 28 October 1861 and had served as Worshipful Master of the Lodge of Lights in 1863. He became Past Grand Deacon in 1869.[224] Worshipful Brother White had also discovered the Warrant of the Jerusalem Encampment granted at York in 1786, which Yarker suggests would have also been carried to Warrington by the Lodge of St. John. The first page of the book is faithfully signed by Yarker, and after a page filled with a cipher key, an index is then presented on the next page under the heading 'Old Lancashire Rituals':

Craft Lectures [pages marked 1-115]
Templar Lectures [pages marked 1-16]
K.T. Priest [pages marked 1-12]
Rosy Cross [pages marked 1-11]
English Templar Kadosh [6 pages not numbered][225]

Immediately following the Craft Lectures on the next two pages, Yarker copied four old Jerusalem banners from the Manchester based Jerusalem Encampment, then he copied the York Warrant and included a very brief history of how it was obtained by Bro. White. Following the York Warrant, Yarker then copied the Templar Lectures and rituals, which will be discussed later.

The Craft Lectures

The book then presents Part 1, Section 1 of the Craft Lectures, and what follows is an array of questions and answers in a typical catechism format, divided up into parts and sections, some of the questions and answers being recognisable to the practicing English Freemason of today, some however, are not so recognisable. These Craft Lectures begin by the Senior Warden being asked 'how did you and I first meet?' The Senior Warden replies 'upon the Square'. From that point, the questions and answers are constantly conveyed, the pages being compacted by Yarker's meticulous handwriting. The text seems to include a concoction of material from ritual and lectures and indeed, as we shall see, the lectures are similar to ones found in the USA. One recognisable sequence for the

1

Part 1. Section 1.

Q. Br. S.W. as Masons, how did you and I first meet?
A. Upon the Square.
Q. Where hope to part?
A. Upon the level.
Q. Why do we meet upon the Square, and part upon the level?
A. As Masons we ought always so to do with all mankind, but more particularly as obligated Brother Masons.
Q. From whence come you?
A. From the W.
Q. Where going?
A. To the E.
Q. What induced you to leave the W. to go to the E.?
A. In search of a Master and from him to gain instruction
Q. Who are you that want instruction?
A. A Free and Accepted Mason.
Q. What kind of Men ought Free and Accepted Masons to be?
A. Free men born of free women, Brother to a King, Fellow to a Prince, and Companions to a Peasant or Beggar if a Mason.
Q. Why Free Men?
A. That the vicious habits of slavery might not contaminate the true principles on which Masonry is founded.
Q. Why born of Free Women?

Library and Museum of Freemasonry

Memoranda of John Smith, in a different hand to the Book.

E. A.

Bk.	ch.	vs.
Genesis.	[illegible]	[illegible]
"	[illegible]	[illegible]
"	[illegible]	[illegible]
"	[illegible]	[illegible]
Leviticus	[illegible]	[illegible]
Deuteronomy	[illegible]	[illegible]
Numbers	[illegible]	[illegible]
Ecclesiastes	[illegible]	[illegible]
Ruth	[illegible]	[illegible]
1st Kings	[illegible]	[illegible]
Isaiah	[illegible]	[illegible]
Matthew	[illegible]	[illegible]
Ecclesiastes	[illegible]	[illegible]
Romans	[illegible]	[illegible]
1st Kings	[illegible]	[illegible]
Jeremiah	[illegible]	[illegible]
Ecclesiasticus	[illegible]	

F. C.

Bk.	ch.	vs.
Exodus	[illegible]	[illegible]
Joshua	[illegible]	[illegible]
"	[illegible]	[illegible]
Judges	[illegible]	[illegible]
1st Kings	[illegible]	[illegible]

M. M.

Bk.	ch.	vs.
Genesis	[illegible]	[illegible]
Exodus	[illegible]	[illegible]
Numbers	[illegible]	[illegible]
Deuteronomy	[illegible]	[illegible]
II Samuel	[illegible]	[illegible]
Joshua	[illegible]	[illegible]
1st Kings	[illegible]	
1 Chronicles	[illegible]	[illegible]
II Chronicles	[illegible]	
Job	[illegible]	
Psalm	[illegible]	[illegible]

Library and Museum of Freemasonry

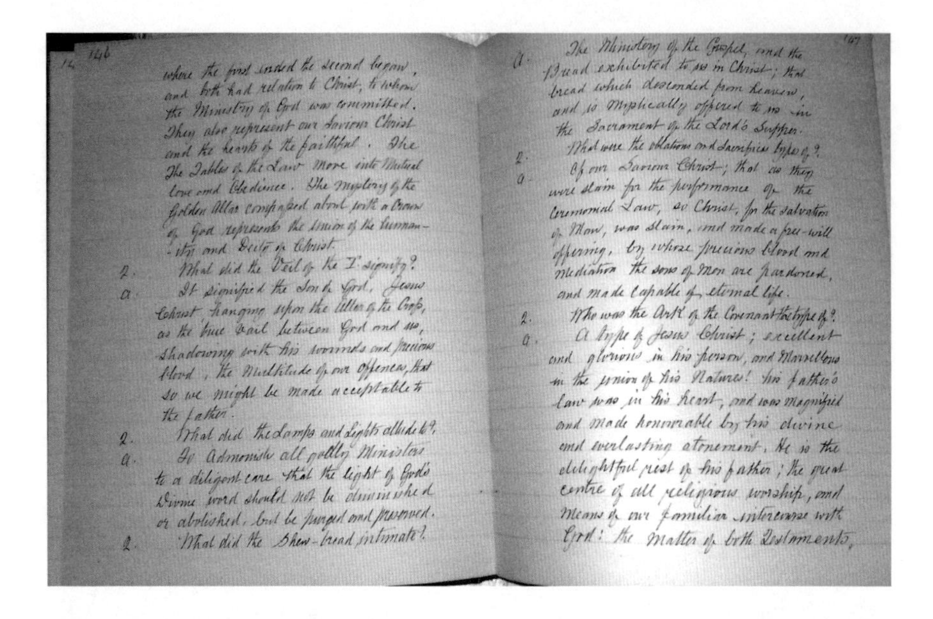

146

where the first ended the second began, and both had relation to Christ, to whom the Ministry of God was committed. They also represent our Saviour Christ and the hearts of the faithful. The Tables of the Law move into Mutual love and Obedience. The Mystery of the Golden Altar compassed about with a Crown of Gold represents the Union of the Human-ity and Deity of Christ.

Q. What did the Veil of the T. signify?

A. It signified the Son of God, Jesus Christ hanging upon the Altar of the Cross, as the true Vail between God and us, shadowing with his wounds and precious blood, the Multitude of our offences, that so we might be made acceptable to the father.

Q. What did the Lamps and Lights allude to?

A. To admonish all godly Ministers to a diligent care that the light of God's Divine word should not be diminished or abolished, but be purged and preserved.

Q. What did the Shew-bread intimate?

147

A. The Ministry of the Gospel, and the Bread exhibited to us in Christ; that bread which descended from heaven, and is mystically offered to us in the Sacrament of the Lord's Supper.

Q. What were the oblations and Sacrifices types of?

A. Of our Saviour Christ; that as they were slain for the performance of the Ceremonial Law, so Christ, for the salvation of Man, was slain, and made a free-will offering, by whose precious blood and mediation the sons of Men are pardoned, and made capable of eternal life.

Q. Who was the Ark of the Covenant the type of?

A. A type of Jesus Christ; excellent and glorious in his person, and Marvellous in the union of his Natures! his father's law was in his heart, and was magnified and made honourable by his divine and everlasting atonement. He is the delightful rest of his father; the great centre of all religious worship, and means of our familiar intercourse with God: the Matter of both Testaments,

Both: Library and Museum of Freemasonry

16

Section III.

Q. Why was you deprived of metals when made a M.?

A. First, that I might bring nothing offensive or defensive into the L to disturb the harmony thereof. 2ndly, As I was then in a State of poverty it was to remind me to relieve all the wants of my fellow creatures without injury to myself or connections. 3rdly, At the building of KST there was not heard the sound of any axe, hammer, or metal tool, throughout that whole building.

Q. Is it possible that so stately and superb an edifice could be finished without the sound of any metal tool?

A. It was, for the stones were hewn in the Quarry, there carved, marked, and numbered; the Timber was felled and prepared in the Forest of Lebanon, there carved, marked, and numbered also; from thence floated down to Joppa, from thence con-veyed to Jerusalem, and there put together, in this wonderful manner, with wooden Mauls, made for that purpose.

Q. Why were metal tools prohibited?

A. That the T. might not be polluted, and that nothing should be heard among the Masons of Zion but harmony and peace.

Q. Why prepared at so great a distance?

A. The better to distinguish the excellency of the Craft, for although prepared at so great a dist-ance, yet when put together at Jerusalem, each part fitted with that perfect exactness as to make it resemble more the work of the Grand Architect of the Universe than that of human skill.

Q. Why was you blindfolded?

A. First, if I had refused to experience the usual Mode of Initiation I might be led out of the L without being able to discover the form or furniture. 2ndly, That my heart might conceive before my eyes could discover; 3rdly, As I was then represented in a State of darkness it was to remind me to keep all the whole creation so, unless they came as lawfully by it, as I did, or was thereafter to be.

Q. Why was you neither barefooted nor shod?

English Mason, with some differences, can be found when a question is put forward:

Q: '*When was you made a Mason?*'
A: '*When the Sun was in its due meridian.*'
Q: '*This seems a paradox, how do you reconcile it?*'
A: '*The Earth being Globular, the Sun is always in its due meridian on some part thereof.*'
Q: '*Where was you made a Mason?*'
A: '*In a just perfect Lodge of Masons.*'[226]

These particular set of questions and answers are indeed similar to the questions put to the candidate at the beginning of the second degree ceremony in the Emulation style ritual used by many English lodges today:

Q: '*Where were you made a Mason?*'
A: '*In the body of a Lodge, just, perfect, and regular.*'
Q: '*And when?*'
A: '*When the Sun was at its meridian.*'
Q: '*In this country Freemasons' Lodges are usually held in the evening; how do you account for that which at first view appears a paradox?*'
A: '*The earth constantly revolving on its axis in its orbit round the Sun and Freemasonry being universally spread over its surface, it necessary follows that the Sun must always be at its meridian with respect to Freemasonry.*'[227]

The ritual copied by Yarker features occurrences of archaic wording, such as 'thereof', 'thereon', 'therein' and 'ye' for example,[228] although modern Emulation ritual has retained evident archaic words. There are also many Christian references that point to the text being pre-union, such as when an answer is given during the first degree 'section' that states 'if we seek for the kingdom of Heaven, we shall find it; if we ask for God's grace, we shall have it, if we knock at the door of mercy with a humble spirit it shall be opened unto us',[229] which can be paralleled to the popular New Testament verse, 'Ask, and it will be given to you; seek, and you will find; knock, and it will be opened to you' found in Mathew 7:7-8. The preceding question and answer to this piece is presented thus:

Q: '*What does these 3 distinct knocks at the door of the L allude to?*'

A: '*A certain passage in scripture, where it is said, seek, and ye will find, ask, and ye shall have, knock, and it shall be opened to you.*'

This is a very similar question and answer structure to what can be found in the second section of the lecture on the first degree in William Morgan's popular exposé *Illustrations of Masonry*, published in 1826 in the USA.[230] The same question and answer and its Biblical reference is also discussed in Edmond Ronayne's *Handbook of Freemasonry*, an exposé of Illinois ritual, the question and answer being featured during an explanation of the first degree lectures.[231] The word 'Amen' is also used besides the familiar term '*So Mote it be*' at the end of the Lectures.[232] Another part of the text concentrates on the working tools, describing them in a similar way to how they are explained today. Some of the symbols are referred to in an overtly Christian context as being representative of eternity, such as the Line which is explained at one stage as 'the never ending circle of eternity…',[233] and the 'Birth, Life, Death, Resurrection and ascension of our Saviour' is mentioned during Section II of the Fellow Craft degree Lectures.[234] Indeed Christ is referred to directly with 'his glorious ascension' being discussed, and named in an exchange during Section VI of the Master Mason Part:

Q. What did the T represent?

A. It represented our Saviour Christ and his Church, for when the son of God suffered the T of his body to be destroyed, & was risen again from the dead, then he raised up to us the Christian Church, which is the true Spiritual house & T wherein God dwells.'[235]

These blatantly Christian references prevail richly through this particular section of the text, with a mention of 'the Deity of Christ' and 'Jesus Christ, hanging upon the Altar of the Cross', giving us a glimpse of the Christian elements that were removed after the union of the Moderns and Antients in 1813.[236]

There are further parallels between the Lancashire Lectures and Morgan's *Illustrations of Masonry*, for example, in the second section of the third degree lecture in *Illustrations* it is declared that:

By the wisdom of King Solomon, who ordered twelve Fellow Crafts to be selected from the band of the workmen, clothed in white gloves and aprons in token of their innocence, and sent three east, three west, three north and three south in search of the ruffians, and if found to bring them forward.[237]

In the *Old Lancashire Craft Lectures*, Part III, section one, a similar answer is given:

> *...went to K.S. with white aprons & gloves as badges of innocence, to acknowledge all they knew concerning it, & voluntarily offered their services to go in search of the 3 assassins...*[238]

Incidents like this shows there is a relationship between the lectures being used in Lancashire in the opening years of the 1800s, and in the New York area by the time the lectures in the Morgan expose were published. The above section also has some semblance with the modern-day English ritual, during the Traditional History presented here during the third degree of a ritual that is used in the Lodge of Lights today:

> *He* [King Solomon] *therefore selected fifteen trusty Fellow Crafts and ordered them to make diligent search after the person of our Master...*[239]
>
> *The same fifteen trusted Fellow Crafts were ordered to attend the funeral, clothed in white aprons and gloves as emblems of their innocence.*[240]

Here, the number of Fellow Crafts involved in the search has changed from twelve to fifteen, the wording has changed and the sequence of events differs, but the symbolism of the white aprons and gloves as emblems of innocence remains the same.

To compare the *Old Lancashire Craft Lectures* with another type of Craft ritual from the same period, perhaps the best rituals to examine are the examples found in the late eighteenth century exposés *Jachin and Boaz* and *Three Distinct Knocks*. However, these two rituals are different to the Old Lancashire Craft Lectures in many ways; the two rituals presented in the exposés describe Table lodges and are also structured differently to the old Lancashire Craft Lectures, which is given as a hand-written catechism split into parts and sections, though the two exposés also feature catechisms in the lectures of the three degrees. There are certainly striking similarities in some of the questions and answers that do suggest a similar source. For example, at the beginning of the Fellow-Craft's Lecture in *Jachin and Boaz*, the Master asks:

How was you prepared to be made a Fellow Craft?'
Ans. I was neither naked, nor clothed, barefoot, not shod...
deprived of all Metal...[241]

The question and answer given is similar to that of the *Old Lancashire Craft Lectures* in Part II Section I:

Q How was you to be passed a F Craft?
A I was neither naked nor clothed, barefooted nor shod.....deprived of metal...[242]

There are differences in grammar and punctuation between the exposés and the *Old Lancashire Craft Lectures*, with the obvious difference being that the Lectures were handwritten by Yarker. Both of the exposés are published works, the rituals are both professionally presented with punctuation and precision, though being printed in the later eighteenth century, certain archaic words are naturally evident.

The *Old Lancashire Craft Lectures* do have some close similarities to the Craft Lectures in the Tunnah Manuscript, especially in the opening sequence of questions, though there are noted differences throughout.[243] Another Craft ritual that has similarities to the Lancashire Craft Lectures is Samuel Prichard's ritual *Masonry Dissected* which was originally published in 1730. Prichard's ritual is presented as a catechism, albeit shorter than the Lancashire Craft Lectures, an example of a similar question and answer sequence can be seen in the third degree of Master Mason in Prichard's exposé:

Q. What are the Master-Jewels?
R. The Porch, Dormer, and Square Pavement.
Q. Explain them?
R. The Porch, the Entering into the Sanctum Sanctorum, the Dormer, the Windows or Lights within, the Square Pavement, the Ground Flooring.[244]

In the Craft Lectures of the *Old Lancashire Rituals* during the Master Mason's part, a similar structure is presented thus:

Q. What are the ornaments of a Master M.L.?
A. Porch, Dormer & Square Pavement.
Q. This How?
A. The Porch is the entrance into the S.S.; The Dormer is the

windows that gives light to the Dorme; The Sq. pavt for the High Priest to walk upon.[245]

The Craft Lectures alludes to many Biblical stories within its catechism structure. In Part I, Section I, the 'Egyptian Bondwoman' is mentioned, which is part of a reference to Hagar and her son Ishmael taken from *The Book of Genesis*, Hagar being guided by an Angel in her despair after being cast out by Abraham.[246] Jacob's Ladder, which is also taken from *The Book of Genesis*, is also discussed thoroughly in a question and answer exchange, 'with the angels of God' being described as '*ascending and descending thereon*', the ladder symbolising the Divine ascent.[247] Both Jacob and Rebecca are mentioned in the dialogue. The Book of Ruth is also referred to in Part I, Section III of the Lectures, the Book presenting the story of how Ruth married Boaz, and how a shoe was given to Boaz to indicate the settlement of a deal were he bought land, and as part of the purchase, Ruth also became his wife. According to the Lectures, this is given in an answer as to why the candidate was 'neither barefoot nor shod' as it was 'a pledge of their fidelity'. It is interesting to see strong feminine characters from the Old Testament feature in the lectures, something that will be discussed in a later chapter when looking at the lost feminine aspects to Freemasonry.[248]

A particular interesting reference can be seen in Part II, Section II, it reads that 'there was a L of Masons held at Alexandria in Egypt, over which Euclid presided…', Euclid and Masonry being mentioned in Anderson's *Constitutions* of 1723 as having 'flourish'd at Alexandria'.[249] The Craft Lectures are indeed an eclectic mixture of ideas that reflect the practice of localised Masonry before the union. With rich Christian and Biblical elements and the use of Anderson's *Constitutions* as a source, the Lectures seem to be a hybrid of Craft catechisms, components of which also appear in various published rituals from throughout the eighteenth century.

Comparisons to the Sheffield Rituals

The Sheffield No.1 MS contains what has been described as the earliest written English version of the Royal Arch ritual, dated to 1780 and written into the first section of a note book. The Sheffield No.2 MS refers to the Knights Templar ritual that was written later into the same book on the remaining pages, probably around 1795-1800. Both MSs comprise what is commonly known as the Sheffield Rituals, which were published in a limited facsimile edition by J.R. Clarke entitled *Early Sheffield Rituals* in

1973. These rituals thus fall into a similar period to that of the Lancashire Rituals, the Sheffield book still being used by 1795-1800 when the Knights Templar ritual was written.[250]

In regards to the Royal Arch ritual which comprises the Sheffield No.1 MS, Christopher Powell puts forward in his paper on the Sheffield Rituals that 'recent evidence suggests that it came from the city of York since the only Moderns' Royal Arch chapter in Yorkshire at the time the ritual was transcribed was the Union Chapter at York', Powell securing a date of 1780 for the binding of the book based on the watermark of the paper. Powell also discusses how the language and syntax of the writing points to a Yorkshire source, and that the ritual has been assessed as being of a Modern origin.[251]

However, there were other early Royal Arch Chapters operating in Yorkshire, most notably in Halifax, where the Chapter of Sincerity was first recorded as being active in 1765. This particular Chapter became dormant for a number of years, only to be revived in 1790.[252] There was also an early Chapter in operation in Wakefield during the 1760s and 1770s, and in York itself, an enquiry into a possible Chapter attached to the York 'Union' Lodge No.236 was discussed in the lodge minutes in 1791. A Chapter was eventually founded by members of the lodge called Unanimity in 1800.[253] The 'Union Chapter' mentioned by Powell was in all probability the Chapter of Unity which was Warranted in 1779, and was attached to the York based Apollo Lodge, a Modern lodge founded by ex-members of the York Grand Lodge in 1773.[254] This certainly fits in with Powell's date of the note book, and could have been purchased in 1780 for the purpose of writing a Royal Arch ritual which was to be used by a Chapter founded the year before. The Knights Templar ritual has also been determined as being of a Modern origin and even though written 15-20 years later by a different hand, points to a continued use of the book as a source for ritual revision and practice.

The Knights Templar Lectures and Rituals

The Knights Templar lectures in the *Old Lancashire Rituals* notebook are indicated by Yarker as being copied from an 1801 copy which had been left by a Wigan brother called Sir Knight Thomas Longsdale Bold. The lectures comprise of sixteen pages, and if the date is correct, then these Knights Templar lectures stand with the Sheffield Knights Templar ritual as being an early example of written ritual from the north of England. Yarker then gives an additional piece of information set in brackets:

> *The Grand Lodge at York revived in 1761 after having been many years dormant, as G.M. Drake was an eminent antiquary he may have introduced some improvements, as their list of officers "three Grand Commanders", differ from those of all other rituals throughout the 3 Kingdoms These are extracts from lectures amongst the papers of the Jerusalem Encampment in 1827, when the system was:- KT or K of St. John 2. Med. Ps. 3. K. of M. 4. K. Rose Croix & Priestly Order...*

Yarker certainly thought these Knight Templar rituals to be unique and to have a link to the York Grand Lodge, and this is where his interest lay; in the secrets of the lost higher degrees of the extinct Grand Lodge. The next ritual presented in the book was originally written down by Jesse Lee in 1839, Lee having been a leading member of Jerusalem Preceptory No. 5 who joined in 1826. Yarker indicates that this KT Priests degree was introduced in 1813, and what follows is approximately twelve pages of meticulously hand-written ritual with symbols and diagrams. There are two additions at the end; an 'Addition from a Ritual of Bro. Leather' on page ten, Brother Leather perhaps being Samuel Leather who joined Jerusalem Preceptory No. 5 in 1858,[255] and a Scottish Obligation on page twelve, bringing this section to a close.

The Knight of White Cross and Knight of the Rosy Cross

Yarker continues his eclectic mix of Templar orientated rituals with a handwritten transcription of the Knight of White Cross and Knight of the Rosy Cross grades, which he indicates was sent to him by a certain Brother Samuel Simpson. The rituals were formerly practiced by a Knights Templar Encampment from Bottoms near Todmorden in Yorkshire, which according to Yarker, was under the York Constitution. Here we have Yarker placing higher degrees together which he surmised were practiced under York. However, the lodge that met at Bottoms near Todmorden was the Prince George Lodge, a lodge first consecrated in 1796 in Haworth, but one that merged with the Lodge of Three Graces in 1809, selling their Warrant and furniture.[256] The lodge re-emerged in 1812 in Bottoms after the Warrant was purchased, and it was this lodge that was linked to the Knights Templar Encampment that Yarker referred to.[257]

The White Cross ritual comprises of four pages while the Rosy Croix ritual covers the following pages numbered one to eleven. What the existence of this ritual does tell us is that the Rosy Cross or Rose Croix was practiced by an Encampment in Yorkshire in the early nineteenth century, though Yarker makes a note observing that 'the Rosy Croix lecture &c, seems to be copied from Carlisle'.[258] Yarker was referring to Richard Carlile's *Manual of Freemasonry*, which does indeed include a description of the Rosicrucian or *Ne Plus Ultra* Degree, the ritual being almost exact to the one that Yarker copied in his notebook.[259] We will examine Carlile's rituals in more depth in a later chapter, but as the rituals were originally published in 1825 and became popular amongst English Freemasons, their use in various parts of the country would not be uncommon. The last ritual presented in the notebook was that of English Templar Kadosh, which came from a different source altogether, a source far from Old Lancashire.

English Templar Kadosh

This final ritual in the notebook comprises of six pages, the ink being darker and the writing finer, but still written in Yarker's recognisable hand. French Mason and writer Ragon is mentioned at the beginning of the introductory title to the ritual, which is written in French:

> *Ragon. Copied un ritual official dilivere par le Grand Conclave d'angletere au Grand Royal Encampment de Port-au-Prince, Republique d'Haiti.*

The jewel is presented as a seven-pointed silver star, and a black eagle with two heads is also mentioned. The letters K.D.S.H are displayed, or *Kadosh*, which is a Hebrew word meaning 'Holy' or 'consecrated', and in placing this Chivalric degree last in his notebook, Yarker was completing his set of rituals. The Knight Kadosh is the thirtieth grade of the Ancient and Accepted Scottish Rite, and Yarker mentions that it differs little from the modern opening, so he was aware of the degree that was practiced at the time of his writing. After this degree, there are a collection of French Cyphers, written in reverse from the back of the notebook, including the Cypher of the Knights Kadosh and some brief notes on the Royal Order of Scotland.

Conclusion

The Craft Lectures included in the *Old Lancashire Rituals* are a handwritten catechism that was once owned by a member of the Lodge of St John No.322, most probably John Smith himself; the book eventually coming under the ownership of the Lodge of Lights after the lodges merged in 1830. At this late stage after the union, the lectures were probably never used in the Lodge of Lights, and being written on a book with watermarked paper dating from 1799, and given a date of c.1802 on Irwin's copy, the pre-union style of lectures were probably used by the Lodge of St John well before the merger. It evidently captured the interest of Yarker who was researching the origins of Freemasonry and the history of his Knights Templar Encampment, and his copy not only presents us with a fascinating insight into a pre-union form of catechism but also allows us to take a glimpse into the mind of Yarker and his obsession with the higher degrees.

Similar lectures were certainly continued in the USA, while, as a whole, being discontinued under the English Constitution after the union. However, certain parts of these lectures, though changed, can be found in the present day English rituals; the questions placed to the candidate at the beginning of the present second degree ceremony and parts of the Traditional History in the third degree being examples of the surviving elements. Yarker's *Old Lancashire Rituals* are indeed as important as the *Sheffield Rituals* in the way that they preserve early versions of ritual practices in the north of England, and certainly are revealing in the way the rituals have evolved.

The Knights Templar lectures and accompanying high degrees appear to originate from a number of different and somewhat varied sources; from a Brother in Wigan, rituals used by the Jerusalem Preceptory No.5 in Manchester of which Yarker was a member at the time, a source in Yorkshire and a version of the Rose Croix taken from Richard Carlile. However, if Yarker is to be believed, these all seem to have been practiced in the north of England during the early nineteenth century, and along with the Sheffield Rituals, they are excellent examples of localised ritual work and progression within Freemasonry. Indeed, there is evidence that Jerusalem Perceptory No.5 did confer higher degrees in the early nineteenth century, including the *Rosae Crucis*,[260] and in Yorkshire, the Encampment in Todmorden also appears to have practiced the Rose Croix degree.

The use of the *Old Lancashire Rituals* certainly reflects the development of the localised Baldwyn Rite in the Bristol area and the Rite of Seven Degrees in London, as examples of independent local Masonic development in England from the 1770s, an interest that can also be seen in how the York Grand Lodge managed a five degree system from the same period. English Freemasons wanted progression, and the supply met the demand. However, these were strictly localised rites and practices, limited to small regions that provided a managed system of advancement within the framework of local Freemasonry. The next chapter examines these localised rites, and how after the union, the ritual in certain English Craft lodges developed particular individual elements and eccentricities, especially after the Liverpool Masonic Rebellion of 1823, something that again reflected the desire for local individuality. Some of these rituals are now in danger of extinction as lodges merge or close in the modern day era, and thus face being lost like the rites of the eighteenth century.

Chapter 5

Ritual Change in England and Wales after the Union of 1813

To be the Table Talk of clubs up stairs...
Poet William Cowper[261]

The higher degrees form the subject of other volumes. They are not common; are dominated by orders of chivalry; and but very few Masons go beyond the Royal Arch Degree.
Richard Carlile[262]

There is some hint of deadlock in the Lodge of Reconciliation in 1815 and there seemed to be a noticeable slowness in the complete adoption by all Lodges of the new Ritual forms.
C.F.W. Dyer[263]

In England, there were what appeared to be localised attempts at managing degree progression, such as in the Grand Lodge of All England held in York, which by the 1770s was practicing five degrees; that of the three Craft degrees, the Royal Arch being the fourth and the Knights Templar being the fifth degree.[264] This York Grand Lodge provided a natural and straightforward progression through these degrees, something that can also be seen with the Wigan Grand Lodge during the nineteenth century; the degree structure being part of the local independent Masonic scene.[265] There were a small number of rites that practiced a seven degree structure, and as we have seen, after the union of 1813, Craft Masonry was changed significantly, though there were subsequent stylised changes in the Craft ritual that took place, again on a localised level. This chapter will examine these localised rites and the local eccentricities of ritual development after the union.

The Rite of Seven Degrees

The Rite of Seven Degrees is a lost rite that operated in England during the

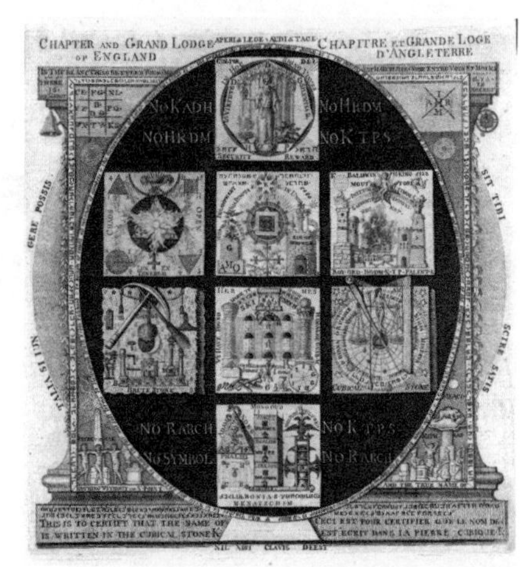

This page and opposite:
A collection of engravings by Peter Lambert de Lintot.
Library and Museum of Freemasonry

NCE
FORTITUDE
SAPIENTIÆ
PLUS
AMOR
NEC
ULTRA
13
14
TEMPERACE
INITIUM
IUSTICE
DOMINI
G
UNA TRIBUS AB UNO
DIEU LE VEUT
SOUVERAINE
METROPOLE LOGE DE LOBSERVLNC
ESPERAGE
CHARITE

OLD AND NEW JERUSALEM BUILDING
FREE MASONRY CROWN'D.
DEDICATED TO THE LEARNED BROTHERS.
London

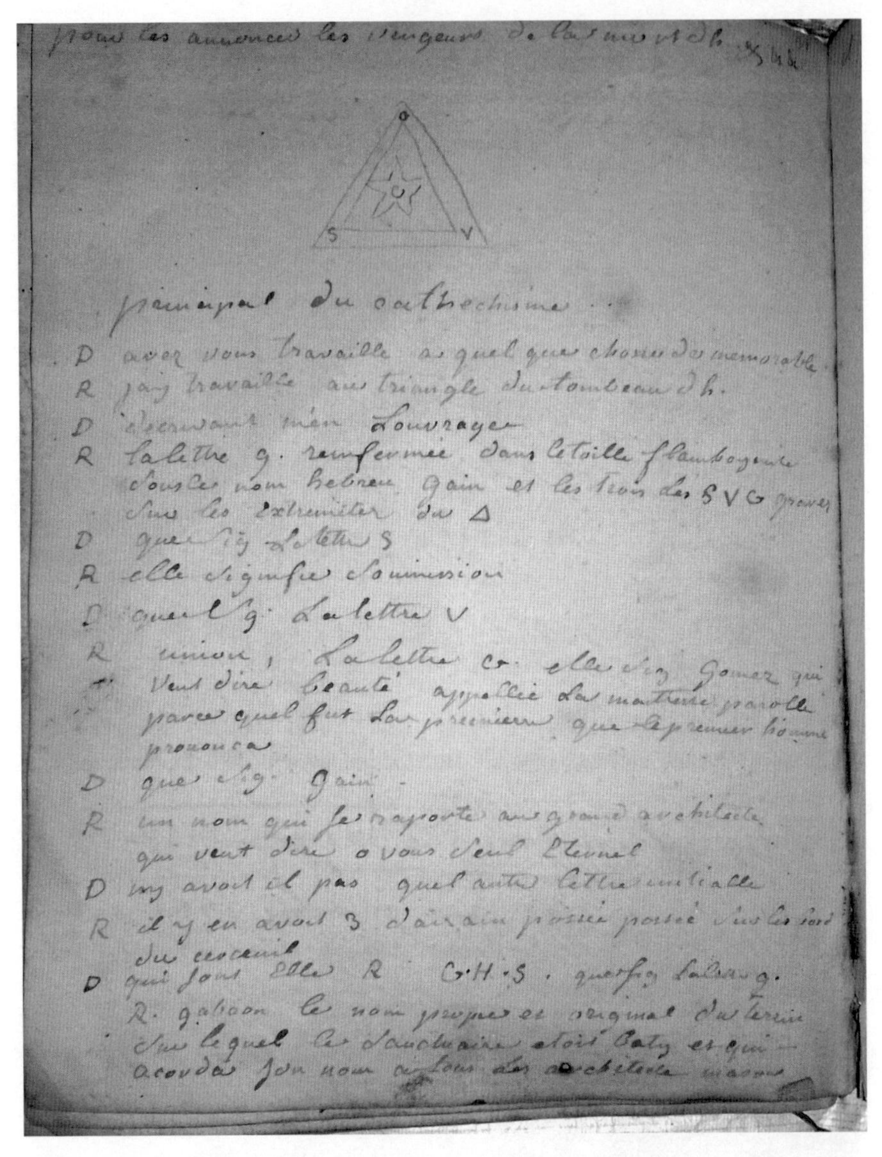
pour les annoncer les vengeurs de la mort de h.

principal du catechisme

D avez vous travaillé a quelque chose de memorable
R j'ay travaillé au triangle du tombeau d'h.
D decrivez mon l'ouvrage
R la lettre g. renfermée dans l'etoille flamboyante
sous le nom hebreu gain et les trois des S V G gravez
sur les extremitez du Δ
D que sig la lettre S
R elle signifie soumission
D que sig. la lettre V
R union, la lettre G. elle sig Gomer qui
veut dire beauté appellée la matiere parolle
parce qu'el fut la premiere que le premier homme
prononca
D que sig. gain.
R un nom qui se raporte au grand architecte
qui veut dire o vous seul Eternel
D n'y avoit il pas quelqu'autre lettre initialle
R il y en avoit 3 d'airain posée posée sur les bord
du cercueil
D qui sont elle R G.H.S. que sig la lettre g.
R. galaad le nom propre et original du terrein
sur lequel le sanctuaire etoit baty et qui
acorda son nom autour des architecte masons

A page from a ritual of the Rite of Seven Degrees, found at the back of the minute book of the French 'Union' Lodge.
Library and Museum of Freemasonry

late eighteenth century and one that had a French influence. The rite was practiced by the Lodge of Perfect Observance No.1, a lodge based in London that operated under the Grand Lodge of England South of the River Trent, a Grand Lodge formed by the guidance of William Preston that came under the sway of the Grand Lodge of All England held at York (1779-1789). The lodge was one of three lodges that operated under this short lived 'spurious' Grand Lodge, but was the only lodge to work the Rite of Seven Degrees, the driving force of the rite being Peter Lambert de Lintot,[266] and according to W. Wonnacott in his article for AQC, there may be 'some things that point to the origin of the Baldwyn Rite', when examining the Rite of Seven Degrees.[267]

The Lodge of Perfect Observance was, on the whole, made up of Frenchman, some having been members of some of the French speaking lodges that met in London. De Lintot had been a Past Master of the Lodge of St. George de l'Observance No.53, and along with his followers, de Lintot had purchased the warrant of French Lodge No.331, which had been constituted in 1765 but was struck-off the list ten years later. After the warrant was purchased, the lodge was given the name 'Union' and a chapter that practiced the higher degrees was connected to the lodge, this going on to become the Lodge of Perfect Observance. De Lintot designed the plates for the Rite, one particular plate forming the frontispiece of the Constitutions of the Lodge of Perfect Observance, and after the Preston schism had ended, the additional degrees were still promoted by the Lodge of St George de l'Observance which was finally erased in 1794.[268]

The Rite of Seven Degrees itself consisted of an elegant collection of high grades that Wannacott suggested originated from the Chapter of Clermont, which after an intense rivalry with an Order known as the Knights of the East, a compromise was reached and an Order called Emperors of the East and West was born. With the high standard of degree work and the noble sounding Chivalric titles, it managed to 'secure ascendency in the G. Lodge de France in 1767' and Wannacott listed seven degrees that were practiced in the Lodge of Perfect Observance, the Union Lodge and the Lodge of St George de l'Observance. These have some similarities to the Rite of Baldwyn, and are presented as thus; the first three degrees are the three Craft degrees, the fourth degree is given the name of Elu, which included a number of un-numbered grades including *Architecte, Prevots et juge*, *Grand Architecte*, *Companion de l'arche Royal*, *Grand Elu*, *Sublime Maitre*, and the final grade of *Parfait eccossois*. The fifth degree was called *Chevalier d'orient et d'occident*, the sixth degree *Chevalier de l'aigle, pelican, Rose Croix de St. André d'heredom triple croix*, or in short *Chevalier Rose Croix*. The seventh and final degree is listed as *K.D.S.H.* Wannacott remarked that there may be other variations in regards to the names of the degrees,[269] but there are certainly similarities to the Baldwyn Rite, especially with the practice of the Rose Croix degree. There are a list of degrees under the Rite of Seven Degrees kept in the archives of the Grand Lodge of Ireland which have marked similarities, with the final degree containing a grade called *Kadosh,* otherwise referred to as the *Knight of the Black Eagle*, which reminds us of Waite's description of the mysterious Rite of the Black Eagle.[270]

The Baldwyn Rite

A rather enduring localised structure can be seen with the Baldwyn Rite, a Rite that is still worked in Bristol in the south-west of England with a degree structure that includes seven degrees. The Baldwyn Rite is certainly part of the localised Masonic scene, but unlike the York and Wigan traditions, it is a structure that has been active within the framework of regular Masonry under the United Grand Lodge of England, and because of its recognition, it has survived. The degree structure includes the first three Craft degrees which are classed collectively as one degree, the next degree is the *Supreme Order of the Holy Royal Arch* and then the Camp of Baldwyn collects the remaining degrees, which includes the third degree of the *Knights of the Nine Elected Masters*, the fourth being the *Ancient Order of Scots Knights Grand Architect*, the *Knights of the East, Sword and Eagle* is presented as the fifth degree, the *Knights of St. John of Jerusalem, Palestine, Rhodes and Malta* is presented as the sixth, and finally the *Knight of the Rose Croix* as the seventh. The rite has a Christian flavor, being named after King Baldwin II of Jerusalem who fought in the First Crusade, being crowned in 1118 and reigning until his death in 1131.

It was just after the beginning of the reign of Baldwin II that the Knights Templars were founded and this association is an integral theme within the rite itself. It has been suggested that the rite has origins in the later eighteenth century, with a Charter of Compact being written in 1780, and there are some similarities to the Rite of Seven Degrees. In 1845, the Knight of the Rose Croix degree was passed to the jurisdiction of the Supreme Council 33° in England, and another Charter of Compact was drawn up in 1862 stating that the Baldwyn Preceptory as a Provincial Grand

Commandery, was given powers by the Grand Conclave of Masonic Knights Templar in England and Wales, to work all knighthood degrees. In 1881, with the claim by the Ancient and Accepted Rite on the Rose Croix degree disputed, it was agreed in a Treaty of Union that the Rose Croix degree as practiced by the Baldwyn Rite was treated as independent. Thus through various charters and treaties, recognition was granted for the Rite to be practiced as a localised system in its own right.[271]

Craft Ritual Change in England after the Union

There had been disputes in Bristol regarding the working of ritual in the wake of the union of 1813, and there had also been a dispute between lodges in Bath. Bath is the location of the Royal Cumberland Lodge, a lodge that boasts a ritual that has strong pre-union elements. The ritual in England and Wales was brought into a standardised format after the union of 1813 and certain ritualistic content, some of which can be found in the previously discussed Lancashire Craft ritual, became disused. A Lodge of Reconciliation was set up in the same year in an attempt to standardise the many varied rituals that had been worked throughout the country under the Antient and the Modern Grand Lodges, and to deal with any disputes that arose. This took some years to implement and had its difficulties, and an Emulation Lodge of Improvement was set up, first meeting in 1823 at Freemasons' Hall in London, enabling the authentic ritual to be practiced and learned accurately '*without permitting alteration*'.[272]

Some lodges sent delegations down to London to learn the new ritual, such as the Lodge of Probity in Halifax, Yorkshire, which sent a number of its brethren to learn the new working, which on their return, they assisted other lodges in Yorkshire to learn.[273] The Grand Master of the United Grand Lodge of England, the Duke of Sussex, also removed the Christian elements from the ritual, best exemplified with the abandonment of the Festivals of St. John in June and December respectively. In the wake of the union the Duke realized that a firm hand was needed to maintain 'order, regularity and the observance of masonic duties'[274] and indeed, the Duke was extremely dismissive of any disagreeable elements within Freemasonry. He had little sympathy for malcontents within the Craft, such being the case with Dr George Oliver, whose removal from his Provincial office was engineered by the Duke after Oliver incurred his dislike.[275]

Rebellion

There was rebellion in Lancashire and from 1823-1913 there was an independent Grand Lodge that eventually settled in Wigan, which continued to practice the 'Antient' ritual; their leading lodge - the Lodge of Sincerity - conducting their ritual in the lodge room around a 16 foot table.[276] This 'Wigan Tradition' effectively practiced a flexible style of working that had been seen during the eighteenth century, with a strong tradition that one of their lodges actually held meetings outside on a canal tow-path, with a Tyler placed at either end of the tow-path to keep out intruders.[277] On the whole however, the transition took place and most other lodges under the United Grand Lodge of England practiced the new ritual, though as a result of the Lancashire rebellion, a regulation change allowed each lodge to regulate their own proceedings, giving each lodge an element of freedom '...that the members present at any lodge have an undoubted right to regulate their own proceedings, provided they are consistent with the general laws and regulations of the Craft'. Thus, during the mid-Victorian period onwards, variations of the ritual emerged locally such as 'Bottomley' in Liverpool and the 'Humber Use' in Hull, and a certain nostalgia developed where certain lodges harked back to a more individual stance that they had before the union, to add their own unique elements to the existing Emulation Ritual, thus creating a distinctive aspect to individual lodge working.[278]

Today, there are around fifty different established Craft rituals or workings throughout England and Wales, and if you include the working of individual lodges, there are countless variations. In the north of England, we have already mentioned the Bottomley Ritual which is worked by a number of lodges in Liverpool and the Wirral, of which there are variations in different lodges,[279] there is the Humber Use which is worked by a number of lodges in Hull,[280] there is the Castle (Northumbrian) Working which also has variations, and of course, the York Working, variations of which are used throughout Yorkshire.[281]

In the south of England, different Craft Workings include the West End Ritual, Hill's North London Working (also known as Taylor's Working), the South London Working, the Oxford Ritual, the Sussex Working, and the Bristol Working, of which there are variations in Bristol lodges. There are many more Craft rituals (far too many to list), but the more common ones include Logic, Stability, Universal, the Veritas Working, the Merchant Navy Working and Claret's Working.[282] There are also many individual lodge workings that are only associated with one particular lodge, such as the Merchants Lodge No.241 in Liverpool and the Lodge of Lights No.148 in Warrington, both having a printed ritual book which has its differences and is strictly adhered to.[283] Another distinct Craft ritual that is now only practiced in just a few lodges is the 'Rose Ritual', a ritual compiled by W. Bro Fredric Rose in 1927 for a group of lodges that met in Warrington, West Lancashire. Calver's Working is another ritual used by a number of lodges in the London area, notably Doric Lodge No.933, and written by W. Bro. Arthur Calver sometime in the early twentieth century.

From the outside these rituals do indeed look like variations of Emulation, with various roles being changed or the odd wording or phrase being added or taken out. In some cases, the perambulation is different, in others certain sections are missed out entirely. However, lodges that work their own ritual are fiercely independent and defensive of their unique ritual working, and it forms part of the particular lodge tradition. In most cases, it does seem that local areas developed their own way of working the ritual during the Victorian era, and formed their own traditional practices. During this time, it was forbidden to put the Emulation Ritual in print, so perhaps with no way of revising the Emulation Ritual other than word-of-mouth, subtle changes were made over a period of years and the wording in certain sections began to get changed slightly due to dialect, and over time it became traditional to a certain lodge. When another lodge was founded in the same area by Masons from a particular Mother lodge, then that same traditional way of working the ritual was passed on.[284]

The Emulation Ritual was only officially published in 1969, so by that time there had been quite a few ritual books privately printed, and these rituals differed slightly from the Emulation Working. George Claret printed an early version of the Craft ritual circa 1836. Claret had attended the Lodge of Reconciliation and his ritual book was based on the Emulation teachings of Peter Gilkes. During the 1880s, the West End, Logic and Oxford rituals were published, and M.M. Taylor's ritual book appeared in 1908. Taylor originally printed it for Henry Hill, who was a member of Marylebone Lodge No.1305, and this became known as Hill's North London Working or Taylor's Working. More recently, an Association was formed to represent the lodges that used Taylor's Working in 1967, and a Taylor's Lodge of Improvement was subsequently held, with a new edition of Taylor's ritual being published. It is very interesting to see the variations of the ritual, and to see the ritual being performed in many different ways, which makes visiting different lodges an entertaining, worthwhile and educational experience.

Similar differences can be found in Scotland; the William Harvey Ritual is popular, a ritual that was born out of concern of the non-Scottish elements that were entering the Scottish ritual. Other Scottish rituals include the Standard Scottish Ritual, which is similar to Harvey's Ritual with a few nuances, the Modern Scottish Ritual, and the MacBride Ritual. Andrew Sommerville MacBride wrote this particular ritual in 1870, and it varies significantly from the Harvey and Standard Rituals, only being used in a few lodges. As in England, there are individual Scottish lodges that have developed their own particular lodge workings and own traditional practices. These many different rituals in English and Scottish lodges are however variations on the same theme, and even if the wording and presentation is different, they all tell the same story within the three degree structure.[285] Some however, as we will see, are in danger of being lost as lodges close or merge and some individual styles of working become redundant, which is what happened to the unique ritual performed by the Lodge of Sincerity when the lodge returned to the United Grand Lodge of England in 1913.

The Rituals of Richard Carlile

Richard Carlile was an English radical of the early nineteenth century, an advocate of free speech and a free press, and an avid exponent of Thomas Paine. Today, Carlile is widely recognised for his paper *The Republican*, and his reporting of the Peterloo Massacre of 1819. The Peterloo Massacre occurred at a reform meeting in St Peter's Fields in Manchester, Lancashire, on 16 August; Carlile was due to speak at the meeting when the yeomanry attacked the crowd, killing 15 people and injuring 400-700 people. It became a defining event in radical British history.[286]

Subsequently, Carlile was imprisoned for three years after being found guilty of blasphemy and seditious libel; he had published a story that had motivated people to hate the government and he had published the work of Thomas Paine that had criticised the Church of England. Carlile was also fined an incredible £1500, and as he could not possibly pay such a hefty sum, he served an additional two years in prison. Despite his Fleet Street premises being raided and shut down, Carlile continued to write for the paper and his wife Jane continued printing *The Republican*, until she herself was imprisoned. Over 150 men and women were imprisoned for selling the paper. His sister Mary then continued publishing the paper until she herself was imprisoned. When Carlile was finally released in 1825, he continued to publish radical material and supported equal rights for women and campaigned for the end of child labour.

In Masonic terms, Carlile is better known for his *Manual of Freemasonry*, an exposé of Masonic rituals that included the three Craft degrees, the Royal Arch, the Mark, the Knight Templar degree and a selection of higher degrees. These high grades included such Masonic morsels as the degree of *Nine Elected Knights*, the degree of the *Priestley Order of Israel*, the degree of *Red Cross Sword of Babylon*, the degree of *Red Cross of Rome and Constantine*, the degree of *Knights of the White Eagle or Pelican*, and the *Rosicrucian or Ne Plus Ultra* degree. This eclectic presentation of high grades not only reveals how the degrees were practiced during the early nineteenth century, but also how Carlile had done a thorough job at researching and documenting them. The exposé was so successful that it was reprinted many times and was used by Freemasons

Carlile's Manual of Freemasonry collected together a version of the Craft ritual, the Royal Arch, Mark, Knights Templar and other high grade rituals. Carlile's ritual was used up until recently in many lodges throughout England and Wales. It is still used in an altered format by Zetland Lodge No 537 in Birkenhead. *From the collection of David Harrison*

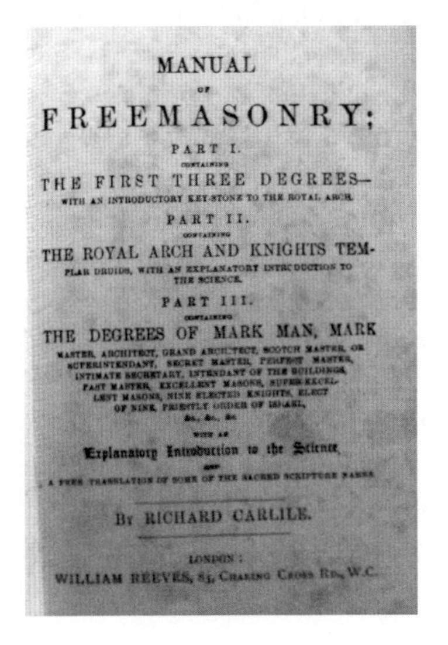

MANUAL
OF
FREEMASONRY;
PART I.
CONTAINING
THE FIRST THREE DEGREES—
WITH AN INTRODUCTORY KEY-STONE TO THE ROYAL ARCH.
PART II.
CONTAINING
THE ROYAL ARCH AND KNIGHTS TEMPLAR DRUIDS, WITH AN EXPLANATORY INTRODUCTION TO THE SCIENCE.
PART III.
CONTAINING
THE DEGREES OF MARK MAN, MARK MASTER, ARCHITECT, GRAND ARCHITECT, SCOTCH MASTER, OR SUPERINTENDANT, SECRET MASTER, PERFECT MASTER, INTIMATE SECRETARY, INTENDANT OF THE BUILDINGS, PAST MASTER, EXCELLENT MASONS, SUPER-EXCELLENT MASONS, NINE ELECTED KNIGHTS, ELECT OF NINE, PRIESTLY ORDER OF ISRAEL, &c., &c., &c.
WITH AN
Explanatory Introduction to the Science
AND
A FREE TRANSLATION OF SOME OF THE SACRED SCRIPTURE NAMES.

BY RICHARD CARLILE.

LONDON:
WILLIAM REEVES, 83, CHARING CROSS RD., W.C.

MANUAL OF FREEMASONRY. 97

The true secret of universal brotherhood must be in equality of knowledge, and honesty of its application. All other pretence is trick, deceit, and inefficiency.—Masonry, in its mysterious ceremony, makes this pretence; but it is a failure, every where a failure, in relation to universality. And it is only by construing the spirit of Masonry to mean a universal equality of knowledge, that its profession of brotherhood can be sustained.

The field of ancient science, which a true knowledge of mythology opens to our view, is the only redemption we have from present superstition. Strong minds, by their own scientific perceptions, may see through superstition; but the multitude of this day is not strong of mind, and wants careful direction to abate its fears, to appease its alarms, and to unfold to its understanding the realities of past, present, and future. Let the Synagogue, the Church, and the Masonic Lodge, become schools for that purpose. Let mystery be sunk by science, and imposture by honesty, that a bleeding and starving world may have some hope of better state in the future of this, instead of being cheated into contentment with ignorance and misery here, under the delusion of attaining happiness hereafter. The immediate present and to-morrow, is that which it becomes man to be earnestly providing for.

This, my playing Knight Templars, is making up the character of a real Christian soldier; and I hope to see and to say—CONSUMMATUM EST.

THE TAU AND THE CROSS.

The Tau is a figure constructed of five lines, thus [symbol], and is considered an important emblem or badge in Royal Arch-Masonry. It is also styled a Triple Tau, or Triple Cross; the Tau of the Greek being like the T of the Egyptian, Roman, or English Alphabet. There were other forms of the Cross. One was the Crux Ansata, thus ♀; another tripled thus [symbol]. In some, there were circles attached to each end thus [symbol] and thus [symbol]; a cross within a circle, thus ⊕. The Roman X,

F

throughout the nineteenth and early twentieth centuries in England and Wales as a source for learning ritual, some lodges actually working the Carlile style of Craft ritual. The *Manual* also became a valuable source for the higher degrees, as we have seen with Yarker's comments in the Old Lancashire Rituals.

Carlile's Craft ritual is in essence a version of Emulation, although there are occurrences throughout of archaic words and phrasing that hint at older sources, an example being a charge that Carlile points out 'is occasionally delivered at the closing of the Lodge by the Master' which begins 'When the Lodge is closed you are at liberty to enjoy yourselves with innocent mirth…'[287] More recently, historian Andrew Prescott remarked that Godfrey Higgins may have been an influence on Carlile's ritual, Higgins being a Freemason who had researched the manuscripts of the recently defunct York Grand Lodge.[288] Indeed, Godfrey Higgins is referred to in the *Manual* as once observing to Carlile 'that there were but two Masons in England – himself and the Duke of Sussex'. Carlile then put in a claim to be a third.[289] Apart from Higgins, whom Carlile had communicated with, influences on his rituals and Masonic writings include the eighteenth century exposé *Jachin and Boaz*, the Masonic works of William Finch, Thomas Paine's *Origins of Freemasonry* and Thomas De Quincey's *Origin of the Rosicrucians and the Free-Masons*.[290] Despite *Jachin and Boaz* as a source, Carlile does not present the Craft ritual within a Table Lodge setting and instead offers a set of degrees that were certainly of his time.

These rituals first appeared in *The Republican* in the latter part of 1825 while he was still in Dorchester Gaol, and Carlile reissued the material in a complete volume in 1831 to accompany the Masonic lectures of his partner the Rev. Robert Taylor. The rituals were reprinted in 1836, and again in 1845, when it was published with the name *The Manual of Freemasonry*. Carlile found himself imprisoned again for printing radical work, and died in 1843. His *Manual of Freemasonry* represents a view of English Freemasonry from the late eighteenth and early nineteenth centuries, but the popularity of his rituals kept them in print continuously for decades, helping English Freemasons with their ritual work well into the twentieth century. Some editions have even been published having the pages sealed together so the ritual could not be read by the casual browser, keeping the higher degrees secret until the time was right.

Table Lodges and the Lost Rituals of *Three Distinct Knocks* and *Jachin and Boaz*

Table Lodges were extremely common in eighteenth century England; they appear in a number of Masonic prints and, as we shall see, feasting and intellectual discussion was part of the bonding of lodge members. Baron Adolph von Knigge introduced the idea of a Table Lodge to the Bavarian Illuminati, the idea perhaps in-keeping with the sense of brotherhood and the increased focus on developing the aesthetic of philosophical conversation within the Order. Indeed, according to Josef Wages in his *School of Wisdom*, Knigge was inspired by a 'Scottish' degree in his possession to introduce the Table Lodge to the Order, the Table Lodge having an overtly Christian flavour that imitated the last-supper and was in effect a celebration of Christian feasting.[291] In England however, these Table Lodges had all but disappeared after the union of 1813.

There have always been festivities attached to lodge meetings, some lodges actually have their meal before the lodge meeting rather than after, and some lodges style themselves as Dining Lodges; lodges that specialise in a more distinguished dining experience. Table lodges were another way of celebrating festivities within a lodge; a table being set up within a tiled

A Table Lodge in the Lodge of Sincerity, the leading lodge under the Wigan Grand Lodge. *Painting by James Miller*

lodge, with food, drinking, smoking, talking and music being an integral part of the lodge meeting and indeed, part of the ritual.

English Masonic tradition has the first Grand Feast being held at the Goose and Gridiron Alehouse in St Paul's Churchyard in London, in 1717 and feasting has since been a central part of Freemasonry, with a special Grand Feast commonly being held on or around the day of St John the Baptist on 24 June and St John the Evangelist on 27 December.[292] The Feast became a central tradition for the assembly of the Premier Grand Lodge in London, though the date on which it was held changed by the early 1730s, fluctuating between March or April. The location for the feast also changed frequently, for example, an assembly and feast took place at Mercers Hall on 17 April 1735, when satirist William Hogarth served as a Grand Steward,[293] on 10 April 1755, the assembly and feast took place at the Drapers Hall[294] and in 1797 the meeting took place at Canonbury Tower, near Islington. A Grand procession to the Grand Feast had also taken place, though this was discontinued in 1745 and the various Provincial Grand Lodges also held a banquet during their meetings.

Before the union of 1813, local lodges, both Antient and Modern, also celebrated St. John the Baptist's Day in June and the day of St. John the Evangelist in December with a feast (the two dates reflecting not only a celebration of Christian feast days, but also dates that were close to the Summer and Winter solstices). In fact, the Grand Lodge of Wigan, which continued the Antient traditions long after the union, persisted in celebrating both of the St. John's days as important feast dates until they re-joined the UGLE in 1913, electing their Grand Lodge Officers on St John the Evangelist Day. The leading lodge of the Wigan Tradition; the Lodge of Sincerity, also met as a Table Lodge, and there is a painting by the last surviving member of the Wigan Grand Lodge James Miller, which shows how the table was set up within the lodge room.[295]

In the eighteenth century exposé *Three Distinct Knocks*, a distinct Table Lodge is described after the floor plan of the lodge is washed out with a mop, and a Table is put in place where the floor drawing was. The brethren then sit down at the table, with the Master sitting at the east, and the senior and junior wardens sitting at the west and south respectively. The exposé then describes how a large bowl of punch, or whatever drink they like, was set in the centre of the table, and the senior deacon then charged in the north and east and the junior deacon charged in the south and west, filling the glasses. The Master then led the toast to the King and Craft, and after the glasses were emptied, they drew the glasses across their throats three times, imitating the penalty of the Obligation of the throat being cut across. They then fired their glasses by slamming them down together, then clapped nine times at the same time as stomping their foot. They then sat down presumably to drink some more.[296]

Another exposé from the late eighteenth century, entitled *Jachin and Boaz*, also describes a Table Lodge within the Craft ritual, and is depicted as having candles set upon the Table in the form of a triangle. The Master is styled wearing a hat and like the Table Lodge described in *Three Distinct Knocks* the Master is sat on the east side of the Table, with the Bible open before him, and the senior and junior wardens are sat at the west and south respectively. The focus on merriment is again suggested when it is indicated that 'On the Table is likewise placed different Sorts of Wine, Punch, &c. to regale the Brethren, who take their Places according to their Degree or Seniority'.[297] With the Brethren seated the lodge is then opened, and after the opening ceremony where the Brethren have to stand, they again sit down and can then 'drink promiscuously, or take a Pipe of Tobacco'.[298]

For the first degree work, a drawing is marked with chalk on the floor at the upper part of the room, the exposé indicating that in some lodges the floor drawing is set out using tape and nails. The fact that the exposé points out on the title page that the ritual is aimed at both Antient and Modern Freemasonry, suggests that the Table Lodge was an integral part of the lodge set-up during the later eighteenth century under both Grand Lodges in England and Wales. The toasting and the drinking was certainly an essential part of the lodge, the exposé indicating that 'the Ceremony of drinking Healths among the Masons, takes up much of their Time…'[299] The Table does indeed appear to have been the central feature in the lodge room, and during the song after the Entered Apprentice's Lecture, the Brethren stand around the Table, holding hands to 'form a Chain' and during the chorus they jumped 'violently with their Feet on the Floor, and shaking their Hands up and down, linked together…keeping exact Time with both'.[300] The drawing of the glass across the throat either before or after drinking is also described as a sign of an Apprentice.[301]

Surviving lodge minutes from the eighteenth century commonly recite how much alcohol was consumed before and after lodge meetings, displaying not only rather large alcohol bills, but reprimands for intoxicated lodge members. The large alcohol bills, along with bills for tobacco, were commonplace, with many lodges having to pay them off at a later date, drinking and smoking amongst the brethren obviously being a vital part of the lodge night. From the many toast lists and Masonic songs that survive from the eighteenth and early nineteenth centuries, drinking, singing and dining was an essential part of the Masonic experience, and for the lodges that used a table in the actual lodge room, there would have been an eclectic mix of ritual, alcohol, feasting and singing. Dining was thus entwined with the essence of Masonic brotherhood, creating a deeper bond between the brethren of the lodge. There is evidence that chamber pots were kept under the table so the brethren could urinate without leaving the room, and indeed, a large chamber pot with Masonic emblems can be seen on display at Weymouth Masonic Hall, the chamber pot being passed around under the dining table, supplying relief for Brethren who had drunk a little too much.[302]

Table Lodges came to an end after the union of Antient and Modern, perhaps because of the Christian overtones of the celebratory feasting. However, the Lodge of Sincerity, the leading lodge under the independent Wigan Grand Lodge, effectively continued the tradition of the Antients in England and held a Table Lodge within a tyled setting. Table lodges do still occur in the US, normally set out in a 'U' shape, whereas in lodges under the UGLE, the festive board which takes place after (or sometimes before) the lodge meeting, seemed to have developed as a separate part of the lodge gathering, held in an un-tiled dining room. The festive board is where the lodge members and guests can eat, drink, toast and talk, but in certain lodges, such as the Harmonic Lodge No.216, a lodge that has met in Liverpool since the late eighteenth century, there is still a remnant of the Table lodge – during their festive board, the working tools are presented to the candidate on the table – giving us a hint of how the Table Lodge once worked.

The York Grand Lodge and the York Working

The York Grand Lodge disappeared in the 1790s, and with its disappearance, its ritual, which included five degrees, was forever lost. However, there is a ritual called the York Working, which is presently used by the York Lodge No.236. The ritual book used by the lodge states that the working is a mixture of the York Grand Lodge, the Antients and the emulation ritual that emerged after the union of 1813. The York 'Union' Lodge was founded in York in 1777, a number of the founding members being 'Antient' Masons, but the lodge was actually constituted as a

'Modern' lodge. It became a bastion to the memory of the York Grand Lodge, welcoming a number of its surviving members who subsequently joined or became regular visitors in the opening years of the nineteenth century, and the lodge is the current custodian of all its documents.[303]

The brethren were still using what they termed as the York Working of the ritual in 1822, when the lodge finally agreed to adopt the new system, as agreed by the Lodge of Reconciliation, which had been set up by the United Grand Lodge after the union. Despite this, the Union Lodge decided to continue the York Working as no member of the lodge had seen the new system demonstrated.[304] The York architectural historian John Browne, who joined the Union Lodge in 1825, was said to be heavily influenced by Antient York Masonry and studied the Antient ritual, ensuring, at least in part, its survival. So, the question remains how much of the present ritual belonged to the ritual of the York Grand Lodge?

The earliest surviving MS of the York Working was written by Brother R.W. Hollon who was initiated in 1841 and became Master in 1850, and a second, slightly different copy exists that was made by a certain Brother William Cowling who was Master in 1855. The York Working was finally put to print in 1924, and the present 'revised' ritual book was printed in

The York Grand Lodge board painted by Thomas Beckwith, showing the York Minster Crypt and an array of symbols, some still current such as the working tools, others such as the pyramids are now lost to English Craft Masonry.
With permission of the York Lodge No. 236

1981. Despite being in effect, a variation of the Emulation ritual, there are archaic elements in the York ritual; old style phrases that seem out of place. However, these old style phrases could still have been used in the nineteenth century – after the union of 1813 and long after the demise of the York Grand Lodge. An example of the use of these archaic phrases can be seen in the York closing of a fellow craft lodge, when the Worshipful Master says: '…His all-seeing eye beholds us; and while we continue to act as faithful Craftsmen….' Instead of the Emulation: '…His all-seeing eye observes us, and whilst we continue to act in conformity with the principles of the Craft…' subtle differences that suggest a more local input perhaps. Perambulations are different also, but as we have seen, in most English lodges it is not uncommon to have different perambulations in different lodges.

In T.W. Hanson's *History of the Lodge of Probity*, which is a lodge based in Halifax in the West Riding of Yorkshire, he puts forward how 'That legendary Old York Working was an excuse, probably invited at this time [1815] for those lodges who neglected to attend the Lodge of Reconciliation'.[305] This attempts to suggest that the York Working was a 'second-hand' variation of Emulation, with 'odd bits' of the old style grafted onto the body of the new, creating a curious blend of styles forged in the early nineteenth century. Whatever its origins, the York Working is a ritual that represents an independent style of working for the York 'Union' Lodge and a handful of other Yorkshire based lodges, such as the De Grey and Ripon Lodge No.837.[306] The present York Working is a ritual that will continue to fascinate researchers, while they forever ponder over the lost ritual of the York Grand Lodge.

Some of the various localised Rituals used in England

Because the Emulation Ritual was not officially put into print until 1969, many aspiring Masons needed assistance in various lodges throughout England and the overseas provinces, to learn and revise the ritual. Thus, many independent editions were printed over the years, some privately by individual lodges, others published because the particular working catered for a number of lodges in a particular area. This led to slight differences in ritual, and led to traditions in certain lodges that did the ritual their own specific way. It may only be slight differences in wording, perambulation, or a certain part delivered by another Officer, but these differences make up a different working, a working that has, over time, become fiercely protected by the lodges that work it. With lodges in England closing or merging, some of these rituals may be in danger of being lost, their peculiarities and particular practices vanishing for ever. We will now examine a number of these 'eccentric' Craft rituals.

The Nigerian Ritual

Every Mason has probably heard the immortal phrase 'this is the way we do it'; a phrase that reverberates with pride in many an English lodge room. The Nigerian Ritual is a well-used ritual in many lodges up and down the country, and indeed, in some of these lodges, they do it differently. From its name, the Nigerian Ritual hints at its origins as a ritual written and published specifically for the Colonial district in Africa in the 1930s, and its name conjures up an image of how English Freemasonry was worked in its jurisdictions within the far flung reaches of the British Empire.

The title page of the Nigerian ritual book reads 'Nigerian Ritual – as taught in Emulation Lodge of Improvement'. The preface written by George M. Gray, District Grand Master of Nigeria in 1939, explained why the District of Nigeria decided to print its own ritual book. On the page it reads that 'The Emulation Lodge of Improvement does not recognise any printed text of its ritual…' which was true at the time and Gray was concerned about the difficulties that arose in the learning and rehearsing of the ritual in his District of Nigeria. A tour of Nigerian lodges took place by W. Brother C.M. Browne and W. Brother Tasker in 1936, and the notes made from the demonstrations on the tour compiled by Browne, who was the Deputy Grand Master of the District and had special experience of Emulation working, eventually resulted in the publication of the Nigerian Ritual book for the use of the lodge members of the District. So, in essence the Nigerian Ritual claimed to be Emulation Working, but with inclusion of meticulous instructions to assist the teaching of the perambulations, such as the strict guideline 'Deacons should carry wands upright and with dignity, never leaned upon or used as walking-sticks.'[307] And thus the correct ritual and procedures could be accessed in printed form in a distant Colonial corner of the Empire.

The book was printed and was purchased by brethren in England also, used as a source for various lodges who adopted this exotic sounding Nigerian Ritual. The ritual, though effectively Emulation, does have subtle differences in its language and presentation; the punctuation is different in places, and some of the wordings are presented differently, and as some lodges adopted it, over time, perambulations became slightly different. The Emulation ritual was finally officially printed in 1969, but some lodges that had been using the Nigerian Ritual since the 1930s decided to stick with the workings that they had been conducting for the past thirty years or so. It thus became a styling of ritual for many lodges, the book being reprinted for them specifically and some lodges printing their own version locally.

The West End Ritual

The West End Ritual appeared in published form around the 1880s, and the tiny ritual book which was passed to me looks very much like a hymn book; with beautiful gold edging on the leaves, each page bordered by red and bound in dark blue fine leather. There are slight differences presented in the wording of the Taylor's Ritual, published in 1908, and the Nigerian Ritual, which was published in 1939. An example can be seen in Taylor's opening of the first degree, when the Junior Warden says:

> *Being armed with a drawn sword to keep off all cowans and intruders to Freemasonry...*[308]

In the Nigerian Ritual, the Junior Warden says:

> *Being armed with a drawn sword to keep off all intruders and Cowans to Masonry...*[309]

Another example of this slight deviation in the practice of ritual can be seen in the questions given to the candidate before the second degree ceremony, the West End Ritual says:

> *Then I will entrust you with a test of merit, which consists of a P.G and P.W...*[310]

In Taylor's Ritual however, the wording is slightly different:

> *Then I will entrust you with a test of merit, which is a P.G and P.W...*[311]

The illustrations of the Tracing Boards also differ in the ritual books; they do not appear at all in the Nigerian Ritual book, the West End Ritual however has beautiful black and white fold out versions on glossy paper, and the Taylor's Ritual book has almost rustic looking black and white etched versions. The perambulations also differ between the rituals and can differ from lodge-to-lodge.

The Bottomley Ritual

As we have seen, the Bottomley Ritual, which is in use in a number of lodges in Liverpool and on the Wirral, emerged in the mid-late nineteenth century. The ritual differs slightly in every lodge that practices it, and the ritual uses more descriptive flourishes and has additional explanations to embellish the working. Each lodge appears to have privately printed its own version of the Bottomley Ritual, with Toxteth Lodge No.1356 printing its own variation for its own members to use. The Liverpool Lodge No.1547, the lodge of William Quilliam, also practices the Bottomley Ritual. This ritual refers candidly to 'Antient Freemasonry', especially in the first degree, and has an almost archaic Victorian fancy to the ceremony, using more flourishes and extended sentences.[312] A number of Bottomley lodges have closed recently, making certain versions obsolete, and recently I came across a lodge in North-Wales; St. Deiniol's Lodge No.3273, which works a version of Craft ritual that is both Bottomley and Nigerian. No current member of the lodge seems to know how this curious merging of ritual came about, but in doing so, it has developed its own unique style of working.

The Humber Use

The 'Humber Use' is a ritual used by a number of lodges in the Hull area of the north-east of England and, like the York Working, is considered an older version of the Craft ritual, with elements that date back to the eighteenth century. It does have archaic elements reflected in certain phrases, and has some noted 'quirks' such as when the Junior Warden is asked by the Worshipful Master in the third degree opening 'Whence come you?', instead of answering from the East, which is common in Emulation ritual and indeed, in all of the other rituals discussed, the 'Humber Use' gives the answer of 'The West', the Junior Warden moving from the opposite direction to search for what is lost.[313]

The Royal Cumberland Ritual

The Royal Cumberland Lodge No.41 is a very early lodge based in Bath that dates from 1733, and it is claimed by the lodge that their Craft ritual dates from at least the late eighteenth century. Their ritual certainly features unique differences, a striking example being that there are four working tools presented to the newly made Master Mason in the third degree instead of the usual three that appear in the Emulation Ritual and indeed the rituals discussed in this chapter. The four working tools presented are 'the Skirrett, the Pencil, the Compasses and the Trowel'. The Trowel is the additional working tool here, used in 'spreading the cement of brotherly love and affection, which ought to unite us into one sacred bond or society of friends…'[314] This is reminiscent of James Miller's description of the Lodge of Sincerity festive board in his *Memoirs*, where a trowel was passed around the brethren with a cry for 'mortar' when a contribution was needed for more drinks. The Lodge of Sincerity was the last surviving lodge under the Wigan Grand Lodge, and the trowel was used here in a similar way; spreading love and harmony in the lodge through drinking and socialising.[315]

Conclusion

In England and Wales, there are local variations that affected the individual styles of Freemasonry and the opportunities for progression, with the development of the Rite of Seven Degrees in London and the Baldwyn Rite in Bristol being examples during the late eighteenth century. This local theme is certainly seen in the development of changes to Craft ritual after the union, as localised workings such as in York, the Bottomley ritual in Merseyside, the Humber Use in Hull and the Castle Working in the North-East, not to mention the variety of London based rituals, reflect how Freemasonry becomes part of the regional identity. Indeed the Grand Lodges of York and of Wigan are further examples of the localisation of Freemasonry, both offering progression within their own Masonic framework. We can only ponder at what the rituals practiced by York and Wigan were like as both Grand Lodges are no more. Yet as lodges close in modern times, many of the individually styled rituals are also threatened with extinction. As some of these lodges have recently closed or have merged, the ritual has thus blended with another and certain wordings or perambulations have changed, the original form being lost forever.[316] There is indeed an element of individuality that makes visiting other lodges more of an event; seeing the degrees performed in a different way being entertaining and diverse.

The third degree Tracing Board of the Royal Cumberland Lodge No. 41, based in Bath. The Tracing Board is described by the lodge as being pre-union and displays certain pre-union symbols that are now uncommon in English Freemasonry in England and Wales, such as the beehive. *With permission of the Royal Cumberland Lodge No. 41.*

Chapter 6

The Lost Archaic Symbols

Virtue has a veil, vice a mask[317]
Freemason Victor Hugo

Isis was the image or representative of the Great Works of the wise men: the Philosopher's Stone, the Elixir of Life, and the Universal Medicine.[318]
Freemason Manly P. Hall

When truth or virtue an affront endures, Th' affront is mine, my friend, and should be yours.[319]
Freemason Alexander Pope

In England, there were certain symbols that disappeared after the union of 1813. Indeed, we have already seen how certain symbolism vanished after particular rites were disused, symbols such as the dagger in the skull that

A rainbow 'banner' depicting scenes from the Fall of Man. York Lodge No. 236.

was said to have been used in the *Maitre Illustre* degree of the Clermont Chapter. Another example of a disused symbol is the bell that appeared in the *explanation of the carpet* in Melissino's Rite, which reminded the brethren 'to be on our guard' and to protect the lodge.[320] The Bavarian Illuminati symbol of the Owl of Minerva could also be considered lost as it belonged to that particular Order which ceased to meet after 1784, as could the symbol of the lion which was used as the emblem of the Scots degree in the Rite of Strict Observance.[321] Other symbols evolved as the particular Rite they were part of evolved, such as the Kneph symbol used for Yarker's Ancient and Primitive Rite that appeared on his journal *The Kneph*. This symbol has now evolved from its original Egyptian stylised form of a winged egg to include other symbols such as the Ouroborus, though *The Kneph* journal also featured other stylised Masonic symbols from time-to-time that reflected the arcane nature of Yarker. The symbol of the Rainbow was once seen as being synonymous with the early Royal Arch, particularly at York, and is a symbol that is now disused in the ceremony.[322] This final chapter of the book will explore an assortment of lost archaic symbols to English Masonry and how other lost rites also used various symbols that have since disappeared from active Masonry.

The Lost Goddess and the Third Pillar

A rather intriguing lost symbolic meaning to a part of the Masonic ritual has been recently discussed by Masonic writer Philip Carter. Carter has put forward that a third pillar in the lodge room is now missing, that which should be related to the Worshipful Master, and that this particular pillar represented a Goddess which symbolised truth, liberty and stability.[323] Indeed, in the eighteenth century exposé *Jachin and Boaz*, the Master asks 'What supports your Lodge?' The answer is given as 'Three great Pillars', the pillars being named 'Wisdom, Strength and Beauty', the pillar of Wisdom representing the Master in the east.[324] This is similar to the three columns that are referred to in the Rosicrucian or Ne Plus Ultra degree; the columns being placed 'with the theological virtues on them, or Faith, Hope, and Charity'.[325]

Three columns are still displayed on the Master Mason's certificate today, showing the Doric, Ionic and Corinthian Orders, and on older certificates when they were sometimes engraved or printed locally during the eighteenth and early nineteenth centuries, they often featured Faith, Hope and Charity personified as women. Faith and Hope were commonly

These do Certify that
the Bearer hereof William Peirce
Has been regularly initiated into the first degree of
Masonry. As such He has been received by Us.
And being a true & faithfull BROTHER is hereby Recommended
to the Favour of all Free and Accepted Masons
wheresoever dispersed.
Given under our Hands and Seal at Boston
New England in St Andrews Lodge Jan 14th AD 1779 &
of Masonry 5779.

Paul Revere M
Wm Hoskins SW
Jona W. Edes JW
Jas Carter Sec

William Peirce

I have caused said brother to affix his Name
in the Margin — J. C. Secy

Engraved Printed & Sold by Paul Revere BOSTON

This certificate shows Faith and Hope standing on the two columned pedestals and Charity is seen seated, nursing a baby accompanied by two other children. Fame is featured at the top of the certificate as a bear-breasted woman blowing a trumpet. It is an example of how feminine figures were featured in a Masonic context in 18th century artwork. The certificate dates from 1779, being printed by Paul Revere.
The Americam Antiquarian Society

seen standing on two of the columned pedestals, Faith holding a book, Hope holding an anchor, and Charity was usually seen seated, nursing a baby and accompanied by two other children. The older certificates also featured Fame as a winged bare-breasted woman blowing a trumpet in the clouds. Another example of a feminine Masonic figure is the portrayal of the Goddess of Architecture on the ceiling of the Blue Velvet Room of Lord Burlington's Chiswick House in London, designed around 1725, and is part of a highly decorative scene that reveals the Goddess residing in the heavens holding a compass, accompanied by three cherubs each holding Masonic tools.[326] Thus there was certainly a feminine aspect to Masonry in a visual sense and a referral to the three pillars in *Jachin and Boaz* and the Rose Croix ritual. However, Carter suggests that this supposed feminine feature within the Masonic ritual was removed at some point in the eighteenth century, but Continental Freemasons enthusiastically picked-up the theme and continued to explore the idea in further degrees, something that soon spread to the US. For example, in the Twenty-Sixth Grade of the Ancient and Accepted Scottish Rite we are told: 'By the altar is a statue or statuette of white marble, the naked figure of a virgin. Over it is a drapery of thin white gauze. This represents Truth, and is the palladium of the Order of Princes of Mercy.'[327]

This theme of the Goddess of Truth, Liberty and Stability enigmatically appeared in French and US Masonic prints during the nineteenth century and can especially be seen with the Masonic dedication of the pedestal of the Statue of Liberty in 1884, the statue being a depiction of the Roman Goddess Libertas.[328] Masonic prints of the 'Grieving Widow' were popular during this time and reveal how Masonry could portray the feminine figure within what was on the whole, a masculine society. This somewhat common imagery of the period normally depicts a Goddess standing on a pedestal, representing a third column, set in-between two other pillars initialled 'J' and 'B', the Goddess sometimes having loose hair, being associated with a virgin, but sometimes depicted as a widow, and occasionally holding a branch of acacia. The image also reminds us of the High Priestess Tarot card as commonly seen in Arthur Edward Waite's famous Tarot deck. Indeed, Albert Pike tells us in his *Morals & Dogma*, Chapter XXIV, 'Prince of the Tabernacle', that:

> *Blue Masonry, ignorant of its import, still retains among its emblems one of a woman weeping over a broken column, holding in her hand a branch of acacia, myrtle, or tamarisk, while Time, we*

> *are told, stands behind her combing out the ringlets of her hair. We need not repeat the vapid and trivial explanation there given, of this representation of Isis, weeping at Byblos, over the column torn from the palace of the King that contained the body of Osiris, while Horus, the God of Time, pours ambrosia on her hair.*[329]

Some of these prints reveal an enthralled but somewhat impoverished crowd surrounding the pedestal, on which the Goddess is standing, who, as stated by Pike, is a representation of Isis. This Goddess brings wisdom and radiance to the people in the crowd, the artwork reminding us of how Freemasonry brings light to the world. Masonic tools and other related symbols can also be seen and the letters 'M B' are displayed on the pedestal signifying the word of the Master Mason and thus associating the image as the lost pillar of the third degree. Isis represents fertility, but Isis was also a widow, mourning the loss of Osiris, who she subsequently resurrected. Like Marianne was a portrayal of the Goddess of Liberty and became a symbol of democracy for the French Republic, the Goddess that was portrayed in the Masonic prints embodied elements of Isis, the Hebrew Goddess Asherah, Reason, Virtue, Veritas and Libertas, to name but a few. Asherah for example is identified with the Asherah Pole, her suggested metaphysical name meaning a pillar, upright and straight.[330] The iconography of these Goddesses are seen in abstract terms, merging to form a feminine Masonic figure on a pedestal in the form of a third pillar. Hints do remain in the ritual, such as when we are informed that Freemasonry embodies 'brotherly love, relief and truth', truth being portrayed as Veritas in various Masonic prints, and as Masons we convey the sacred dictates of 'Truth, Honour, and of Virtue'.[331]

Indeed, Truth is often seen with a mirror, reflecting the truth of one's self, one's inner feelings that we sometimes bury deep inside. This is something that is examined in the

Left and Above: A monument to a deceased Freemason, the symbol of the broken pillar in Freemasonry was quite common and can be seen in many eighteenth and nineteenth century Masonic prints. This is a monument in a graveyard in Anglesey, North Wales dating from 1902.

Time and Truth as displayed on a fresco in the library of the late nineteenth century Ullet Road Unitarian Chapel in Liverpool.

Chamber of Reflection, a process that the candidate had to undergo in Cagliostro's Egyptian Rite.[332] In this chamber the candidate would be 'made to understand how painful is the path of philosophy and how crowded with dangers and troubles…'[333] The 'brother terrible' is also featured here to take details from the candidate to give to the Master, this being similar to the 'Terrible Brother' that is featured in the fourth degree of the Melissino Rite – the Dark Vault. The Dark Vault is a similar reflective chamber where the 'Terrible Brother must test the candidate most rigorously…'[334] This way, the truth is accessed and, as symbolised by the Goddess of Truth, the candidate understands his reasons for joining the Order and can examine them thoroughly. As we have seen in Cagliostro's Egyptian Rite, women could also join, and a 'co-Masonic' spirit was promoted.

A somewhat abstract blend of ancient female Deities merged to create a unique Masonic Goddess that was sometimes represented as a virgin, and sometimes as a widow. This strong feminine imagery can also be seen with the broken column – a symbol that can be found in many Masonic prints during the nineteenth century, and a symbol that also appeared as the emblem of the Apprentice degree in the Rite of Strict Observance.[335] The image of the broken column is said to symbolise the fall of Hiram Abiff and the incomplete Temple as a result of his fall, something that is explained in the third degree. In the Strict Observance ritual when discussing the symbol on the Apprentices' tracing board, it is indicated that 'the most distinguished and greatest part of the Order was smashed and thrown down like the chapter of the pillar through the destruction of Philippo Pulchro [Philip the Fair], the foundation nonetheless remained, because it kept on being propagated in secrecy'.[336]

Thus the broken column indicates a life that has been cut short, and the weeping widow mourns for the loss of her son, Hiram Abiff. Time can also be viewed in the imagery, reminding us of mortality, something that is also taught in the third degree ritual and will be examined further. As Francis Bacon once said 'Truth is rightly named the daughter of time, not of authority', a rather apt quotation in regards to the search for the lost word, which is eventually found during the Royal Arch ritual, a ritual that in England, completes the third degree, and one that is set years after the destruction of the Temple. The Masonic ritual certainly conveys sets of three, and a third pillar within the ritual would indeed make sense, and though this image of the sacred feminine disappeared, the words of truth, liberty and stability remain as powerful as ever.

J
B
M B

Mercury and Caduceus

In England, the union of the Moderns and Antients in 1813 led to changes in the ritual that resulted in the loss of certain symbols, Yarker commenting in his *Arcane Schools* that 'all Christian references were expunged'.[337] The same seems to have happened to the more esoteric symbols within the Craft in English and Wales, symbols that were also common in alchemy and were featured in some of the lost rites we have been discussing. One such powerful symbol was of Mercury and Caduceus. Mercury was the messenger of Jove, known for his speed and mobility, which obviously resounds in the work of Junior Deacon, and also that of the Senior Deacon in the lodge; the Junior Deacon carries the messages and communications punctually from the Senior Warden to the Junior Warden, and the Senior Deacon bears the messages and commands from the Worshipful Master to the Senior Warden.

Mercury was also a symbol used in alchemy, Mercury being able to bring the dead back to life – *the Quick and the Dead* – something which reflects the themes portrayed in the third degree and indeed, the Staff of Mercury appeared prominently on the tracing board of the Master degree in Cagliostro's Egyptian Rite.[338] Mercury can also be seen adorning the ceiling of the Red Velvet Room in Lord Burlington's Chiswick House, the image, according to historian Ricky Pound, reflecting Burlington's close

Title: A. La Maçonnerie Secourant L'Humanité (Masonry Saving Humanity) 19th C., Augustin M. lith., Lith. Fourquemin, Paris, chez Kiener, Place Maubert, 41.

The female personification of Freemasonry is presented here as the Goddess of Truth, surmounted by a five-pointed star. The letters on the two pillars show them to belong to the first and second degrees, while the Goddess stands on a pedestal bearing the initials 'M' and 'B,' signifying the word of a Master Mason and revealing her to be part of the pillar properly belonging to that degree. At the base of the pedestal are a hammer and shattered chain, signifying her liberation, together with a broken demonic mask, suggesting her true nature is no longer hidden. *Courtesy of The Masonic Library and Museum of Pennsylvania*

The text accompanying the image reads:
Elle aide l'infortune et tarit tous les pleurs: 'veuves, enfants, vieillards en elle out un refuge.
De'elle vient la lumiére, et, la prenant pour juge l'esclave lui demande un term á ses douleurs.

Masonic associations.[339] The legend recites how Mercury was in possession of an Olive branch wand that he used to separate two serpents in combat, hence the wand *Caduceus* became a symbol of peace, which resounds in the present symbol of the dove carrying an olive branch, used by the Deacons working in lodges founded after 1813, and perhaps resonates in the fact that both Deacons use wands.

In alchemy, an early science that was practiced by seventeenth century Freemasons Elias Ashmole and Sir Robert Moray, the element of mercury represents movement, fluidity, flux and transformation, and is sometimes known as quicksilver. In ancient China, mercury was thought to be able to prolong life, and the alchemists of the early modern period believed that gold could be produced by varying the quality and quantity of sulphur contained in the mercury. We have already seen how Cagliostro married Freemasonry and alchemy in his Egyptian Rite, which has been seen as having elements of both science and religion.[340]

Another early influential Freemason who was certainly aware of such areas of research was the natural philosopher Dr Jean Theophilus Desaguliers. Desaguliers was an avid 'disciple' of Sir Isaac Newton and had been charged by his patron the Duke of Chandos in 1732, to enquire

The silver Mercury and Caduceus symbol used by the Deacons of the Lodge of Lights No. 148 in the West Lancashire Province of the UGLE. The lodge was founded in 1765 and was allowed to keep the jewel after the union of 1813.

into the work of the mysterious Baron Silburghe, who had 'found out a secret of fixing quicksilver'.[341] Mercury was thus extremely important to early alchemists and early Freemasons, and it is very apt that the wands of the two Deacons are symbolic of Mercury, enabling them move freely and promptly in the lodge room to convey messages and to guide the candidates on their Masonic journey, which ends in their rebirth as Master Masons. In England and Wales, pre-union lodges were allowed to keep the symbol, and some of these lodges still use the Mercury and Caduceus symbol today.

Tempus Fugit (Time Flies)

The winged hourglass has appeared in many eighteenth century Masonic exposés and on early tracing boards. The symbol represents mortality; the sands of time slipping away to the bottom of the glass, reminding us that we are only on this Earth for but a short time. The symbol suggests to us that *Time flies* – and the symbol can be placed next to the many other symbols of mortality such as the skull and crossbones, the scythe, and the coffin to compound this theme. However, the hourglass can be turned over, and the sands of times can once more run through the glass. It was once a popular image on gravestones in the seventeenth and eighteenth centuries, the hourglass itself appeared as a symbol for Friendly Societies such as the Free Gardeners and the Independent Order of Oddfellows,[342] and it also appeared in artwork associated with alchemists, magic and the mystery of hidden knowledge, such as can be seen in Albrecht Dürer's *Melencolia I*, which dates from 1514.

On the Master degree tracing board of Cagliostro's Egyptian Rite, the inverted hourglass appears with a broken scythe of Time, the board itself being dominated by images and symbols of mortality; Time is featured 'in the form of an old man, big and strong, having two large wings'. A Master Mason also appears on the board with a sword in his right hand, seemingly ready 'to strike or cut the wings of time'; reminding us that death can strike at any time.[343] This is the same image of Time as an old man with wings, holding a scythe in his left hand, expressing terror and 'having an hour-glass on his head' that the candidate encounters first on entering the Chamber of Reflection.[344] It is this common image of Time that appears with the Goddess of Truth, and indeed the purpose of the chamber is so the candidate can reflect upon his inner self.

Evidence for the use of the hourglass as a powerful pre-union Masonic symbol, along with many other now disused lodge symbols in England such as the beehive, anchor and ark, can be found in the memoirs of James Miller – the last surviving member of the Wigan Grand Lodge, which were the last remnants of the Antients in England. The Wigan Grand Lodge emerged from the Liverpool Masonic Rebellion of 1823, which was a reaction against the union, and continued to exist until 1913. Miller wrote about the tracing board used in the ritual:

> *I only remember one tracing board, it was a piece of canvas about 4ft square. On it were painted the three steps; pot of incense; Beehive; book of constitutions with tylers sword; All seeing eye; sword pointing to a naked heart; Anchor and Ark; Forty seventh problem of Euclid; Hour glass and scythe…*[345]

Most of the symbols mentioned by Miller are also presented in Thomas Smith Webb's early nineteenth century US publication the *Freemason's Monitor*, almost in the same order.[346] A similar display of symbols including the pot of incense and the enigmatic 'sword pointing to a naked heart' can also be seen on the pre-union third degree tracing board of the Royal Cumberland Lodge. The pot of incense is described by Webb as 'an emblem of a pure heart, which is always an acceptable sacrifice to the Deity', the sword pointing to a naked heart reminding us that 'justice will sooner or later overtake us…' both emblems reminding us of the powerful moralistic and spiritual themes that can be found in the accompanying symbols.[347] A pot of incense was also described as being used in the magical ritual of the Rite de Elus Coens; a small earthenware dish containing hot coals was carried by the adept, the ingredients of the mixture in the dish being said to contain saffron, incense, white and black poppy seeds, nutmeg and spore of agaric.[348]

The Ark

The Ark symbol within English Craft Freemasonry, like the beehive, became disused in the lodge room after the union in 1813, perhaps because of its obvious Biblical connection, although, along with the beehive, it was still used by the Grand Lodge of Wigan which practiced a form of the Antient ritual, and as we have seen above, both symbols appeared on the tracing board for the Lodge of Sincerity, the main lodge of the Wigan based Grand Lodge.[349] Interestingly, both the beehive and the Ark and anchor appear on the third degree Tracing Board of the Royal Cumberland Lodge, being mentioned in their ritual, which, as we have seen, is considered by the lodge to be pre-union.[350] The Ark is usually combined with an anchor, and together they are symbols of well-spent life; the Ark being a symbol of faith, and the anchor a symbol of hope, hence the large number of English lodges that have 'faith' and 'hope' in their name.

The Ark, like the Temple, is a sanctuary, and along with the anchor keeps us 'sure and steadfast', a motto that is used by the Boys Brigade movement; a movement that is much celebrated in some English and Welsh Masonic lodges.[351] In a Charge delivered to the constitution of a lodge in Wolverhampton by the Grand Master Pro Tempore in 1764, Noah and 'the great Fabric of the Ark', is described as being 'built by God's appointment, to preserve the few faithful of all the Antediluvians', reinforcing how God's design of the Ark was venerated within eighteenth century English Craft Freemasonry.[352] The Ark also appeared as a symbol for various Friendly Societies in the nineteenth century such as the Loyal United Free Mechanics and the Free Gardeners, societies that also used an array of more 'rustic' symbols found in pre-union Freemasonry such as the beehive.[353] The moralistic and Biblical imagery of the Ark is striking, and also reminds us that the Ark was constructed with instructions from God, and like the beehive, the symbol remained popular in American Freemasonry, being mentioned in Webb's *Freemason's Monitor*.[354] It survives in England and Wales as the main symbol of the Royal Ark Mariner Degree, a symbol that also features the rainbow.

The Ouroboros and symbol of infinity

The snake in a 'figure-of-eight' position is similar to the symbol of infinity, a never-ending flux without any limit, which again reflects the theme of immortality within Freemasonry; the Master Mason rising from the figurative grave during the third degree. The symbol of infinity appears within English Freemasonry as early as the eighteenth century, appearing for example in a print of various Masonic symbols in the 1769 edition of *The Book of Constitutions*. The concept of the nature of infinity has its roots in ancient Greek and Indian philosophy, though the symbol itself is often accredited to the seventeenth century English mathematician John Wallis, who was part of a group of natural philosophers that evolved into the Royal Society. The symbol is used within mathematics denoting an unbounded limit.[355]

The image of the snake itself has featured in Christian art for centuries,

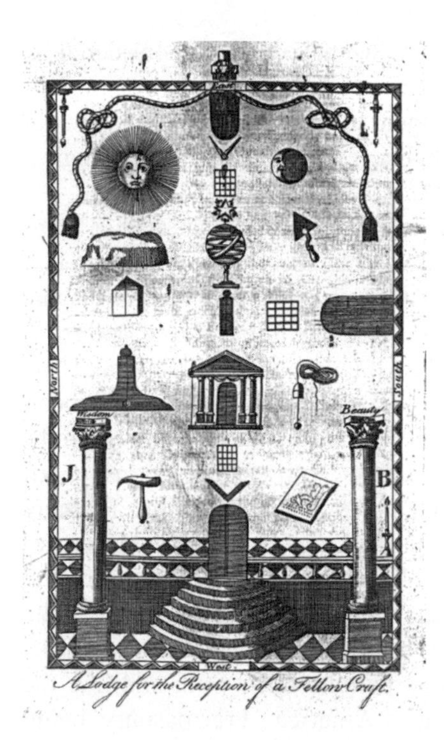

A print from the 1769 edition of the *Constitutions* showing various symbols including the symbol of infinity. The infinity symbol can be seen as the plumb line wound in a figure-of-eight.
Care of the Warrington Masonic Museum

commonly depicted as the serpent coiled around the tree of knowledge that appears to the wife of Adam in Genesis, beguiling her to eat from the tree, and then giving the fruit to Adam which procures them forbidden knowledge and signifies the Fall of Man. The serpent became a powerful symbol, conjuring up fear and representing hidden knowledge, and

This stylised ouroborus is taken from John Yarker's publication *The Kneph.*

especially denoted fertility, medicine and regeneration in certain cultures. In the late eighteenth century Masonic sermon by the Rev. Harris, certain Masonic emblems were explained, and it was observed of serpents 'that they cast off their old skins in the Spring, and a new one succeeds them, and they grow, as it were young again. It may be proper for us, in imitation of this, to throw aside our rough exterior, and become smooth, pliant, and insinuating'. In essence, the snake was being seen as the entered apprentice, with 'the superfluous matter which must be knocked off' symbolising the rough skin being shed and the apprentice growing in skill.[356]

As a symbol of life, death and rebirth, the Ouroboros symbol - the snake eating its own tail - can be traced to Ancient Egypt and occurs in many other cultures, such as in Norse mythology, where it appears as *Jörmungandr*. The enigmatic image of the Ouroboros was adopted by the alchemists of the early modern period; its circular representation of eternal life and infinity being alluded to in Hermetic works of the seventeenth century such as *The Garden of Cyrus* by Thomas Browne.[357] Like the infinity symbol, the Ouroboros was found frequently within the Masonic framework during the eighteenth century, finding a home next to other symbols of life, death and rebirth. An example of its use can be seen on the York townhouse of the Grand Master of the Grand Lodge of All England held at York, Charles Bathurst. Bathurst was the Grand Master of York in 1726, and the Ouroboros can be seen a number of times on the downspout of his townhouse in Micklegate in York.[358]

We have seen how the image of the snake appeared a number of times in association with Cagliostro's Egyptian Rite; there was a serpent in the Chamber of Reflection,[359] Cagliostro himself held a 'serpent rod' during the ceremony[360] and the overtly comical image of the naked Cagliostro clasping a snake in his hand as he was supposedly lowered from the ceiling of the lodge.[361] This of course provides us with a sexual image for the snake set within Cagliostro's form of Freemasonry and reminds us of the Libertine overtones of the period. However, according to Faulks and Cooper in their work on Cagliostro, he did use the Ouroborus in the context of Freemasonry, sketching the symbol while exchanging Masonic signs with a traveller.[362] The symbol occurred on the York Lodge 'service' certificate which dates from the nineteenth century, and currently survives on the centenary jewel of the UGLE.[363] The Ouroborus still appears as a main symbol for the Ancient and Primitive Rite of Memphis-Misraïm and also appears on the seal for the Theosophical Society. The symbol was also used

Masonic Chair from the late eighteenth century again showing the beehive symbol.
Derby Masonic Hall

by Eliphas Lévi in his *Great Seal of Solomon*. The Ouroborus was indeed a highly significant symbol that embodied the infinity of the cycle of life, death and rebirth, and thus reflected the central themes of both Freemasonry and the Western Esoteric Tradition.

The Beehive Symbol

The beehive is one of Freemasonry's most enigmatic symbols and can be seen in an early Masonic print dating to 1755, displayed with a wide variety of now lost symbols, but the earliest known possible Masonic reference to the beehive is found in an MS entitled *A Letter from the Grand Mistress of the Female Free-Masons to Mr Harding the Printer,* found in the Halliday Collection, Royal Irish Academy, Dublin. The document is believed to have been written in the 1720s and while originally attributed to Freemason and satirist Jonathan Swift, the true author remains unknown. The manuscript identifies Bees with Masonry in a strong symbolic sense:

> *Masonry or Building, seemeth to be of the very Essence or Nature of the Bee, for her building not the ordinary Way of all other living Creatures, is the generative Cause which produceth the young ones...What Modern Masons call a Lodge was for the above Reasons, by Antiquity call'd a HIVE of Free Masons. And, for the*

> *same Reasons, when a Dissention happens in a Lodge, the going off and forming another Lodge, is to this Day called SWARMING.*[364]

The beehive features enigmatically in the ritual of the Royal Cumberland Lodge No.41, a lodge that was founded in 1733, in Bath, Somerset. The

A Masonic print found in an edition of Christopher Wren's *Parentalia* dating from 1755 showing a variety of lost symbols, including the beehive. *Library and Museum of Freemasonry*

lodge is a very early lodge indeed, and it still uses a ritual which, it is claimed, is pre-union. The beehive also takes a prominent position on the third degree tracing board of the Royal Cumberland Lodge which also dates from before the union. The symbol does appear on a number of other pre-union boards from various lodges in England according to Masonic historian George Bullamore, some being first degree tracing boards,[365] so we can say that the beehive was referred to in the ritual.

The beehive is also famously mentioned in Thomas Smith Webb's *Freemason's Monitor*, published in the USA during the opening years of the nineteenth century, where a detailed description is given of its meaning, part of which is very similar indeed to part of the description given of the beehive in the Royal Cumberland ritual:

> *The Beehive teaches us that as we are born into the world rational and intelligent beings, so ought we also to be industrious ones...*[366]

And the Webb version in comparison:

> *It teaches us that we came into the world rational and intelligent beings, so we should ever be industrious ones...*[367]

Thus the symbol survived in the USA, where it subsequently appeared on Master's Carpets and in lectures, and appearing in William Morgan's *Illustrations of Masonry* as an emblem of the third degree.[368] The symbol represents industry and the working lodge. Seven bees are usually seen flying around the hive, seven being the number of Freemasons to make a perfect lodge. The beehive symbol was adopted by many Friendly Societies during the nineteenth century such as the Independent Order of Oddfellows, and by Trade Unions and insurance companies, the hive representing industry and the bees the workers.[369] The beehive is thus a traditional image, with almost rustic and working-class connotations, and this may explain why it was dropped from the collection of symbols of science, geometry and precision that now dominates the modern Freemasonry of the UGLE.

It also survived as a symbol in the Wigan Grand Lodge, appearing on their tracing board according to Miller, and can still be seen in some pre-union lodges, appearing on lodge furniture such as on a chair in the Lodge of Probity in Halifax and on a Masonic chair displayed at Derbyshire Masonic Hall. The Lodge of Probity also features the beehive on their lodge summons, which is printed from a pre-union plate. The symbol also appears on various Masonic ceramics that can be found on display in Masonic museums across England, such as the pre-union Masonic jug at the Warrington Masonic Museum. Apart from being shown on furniture, ceramics and on rare tracing boards from various pre-union lodges, the beehive symbol disappeared from English and Welsh lodges, though a model of the beehive was still used by Waveney Lodge No.929 in Suffolk, a lodge that only dates from 1862. It still remains perhaps the most enigmatic and rustic of all the lost Masonic symbols.

Conclusion

These lost archaic symbols are remnants of older practices, some are Christian, some are magical, and they represented the blend of beliefs that made up Freemasonry. The paradigms and concepts of the various types of Freemasonry and high grades that have been discussed here reveal a complex array of symbolism that seem to reflect the journey of the candidate to Master Mason and indeed, beyond. The occurrence of Time seen at the entrance of the Chamber of Reflection in Cagliostro's Rite, the hidden references to Truth, and again being reminded of the essence of Time in the Master Masons degree, all mirror the cycle of life, death and rebirth within the Rite. This intricate theme can be seen with the use of the Ouroboros and the symbol of infinity, symbols used in alchemy, which is indeed a central concept in Cagliostro's Egyptian Rite. The idea of the lost Goddess as a Masonic symbol also reminds us of possible feminine concepts within Freemasonry in the past, and indeed it could be suggested that ancient Goddesses such as Truth and Virtue have impacted upon our modern ritual, the value and meaning of the words containing depths within the central themes of the ritual. As Freemasonry has changed over the centuries, the ritual and the symbolism has also been changed, but these central themes remain the same. Indeed, symbols such as the beehive, the Ark and Mercury with Caduceus were disused after the union in England, and though some survive in older lodges as antiquated features of a distant Masonic past, on the whole these symbols became archaic and redundant as concepts were revised. Despite the development of modern ideas, the older message is still retained, hidden behind the veil and embedded within the allegory.

Lost Rites and Rituals of Freemasonry: Conclusion

The lost rites of the eighteenth century were a reaction to the fashion of Freemasonry that swept the Continent at that time; rites created by charismatic gentlemen such as Count Cagliostro, Baron von Hund and Melissino, who constructed intricate rituals and for a time, attracted quite a dedicated following. The arcane nature of some of the lost rites certainly reflects the way that the secret practice of Angelic and spiritual communication was an integral part of the teachings within the particular rite. The teachings of Pasqually in the Rite de Elus Coens are perhaps the best example of this practice of spiritual communication, along with the Angelic communications that are discussed in Cagliostro's ritual and the hints of spiritualism that may have taken place with members of the Order of the Rosy Cross. The search for the lost word of God that we still see today performed in the theatre of Craft Freemasonry and the Royal Arch, was boldly taken a step further in these rites, with Angelic communication being attempted in the search to gain hidden knowledge.

These lost rites, nearly all of which stopped working as the eighteenth century came to a close, captivated many leading Freemasons and occultists during the occult revival of the later nineteenth century, some like John Yarker, F.G. Irwin and Papus, 'reviving' rites such as the Swedenborgian Rite, Fratres Lucis and Martinism during a period of renewed interest. There was however a lack of continuity with the original rite and when the particular rite was revived, it was done so with attempts to reconstruct it from surviving notebooks or with ideas perceived by men like Yarker or Papus, recreating the rite in a new fashion that reflected the era they lived in. The Antient and Primitive Rite was an example of a rite in progression; formed from the merged Rites of Memphis and Misraïm, refined and then promoted by the likes of John Yarker. It was said to have originated from Cagliostro's Egyptian brand of Freemasonry by Mackenzie, but Yarker promoted a version that was refined and adapted.

Among these lost rites are included truly obscure Orders, such as the Rite of the Black Brethren and the Rite of the Elected Cowans, rites that we know very little of. Others, like Cagliostro's Egyptian Rite, we do have the ritual for, but it can still be considered lost in the sense that we do not know exactly how it was performed or practiced; the use of a medium in the ceremony procedure, possible sexual overtones and the speculative use of DMT within the ritual testify not only to the fascination of the rite for modern researchers, but to the fact that we have little understanding of its true nature. As Waite suggested in his work on Saint-Martin, the precise teachings of Pasqually are not known, and thus we have to speculate on the whole nature of the rituals, its process and how the results of the spiritual communication were analysed and interpreted. These teachings did however go on to inspire occultists such as Papus and the work can be reflected in the scrying and séance work conducted by Freemasons such as Frederick Hockley and F.G. Irwin during the occult revival, Irwin going on to recreate a version of Fratres Lucis from supposedly contacting Cagliostro during his scrying sessions. Hockley and Irwin, like Pasqually, Willermoz and Saint-Martin before them, were very intelligent and highly respected men, Hockley was a Grand Lodge Officer and Irwin had gained respect from the likes of R.F. Gould and Sir Charles Warren both as a soldier and a Freemason. These gentlemen certainly believed in their spiritual endeavours, and like Frederick Bligh Bond and Sir Arthur Conan Doyle, embraced spiritualism as a means to search for hidden knowledge.

The union of 1813 had a seismic effect on Masonic ritual in England, the ceremony and the accompanying lectures were transformed, with Craft lecture systems like the ones seen in the Old Lancashire Rituals being abandoned. The Table Lodges that were popular in the eighteenth century became redundant, certain symbols were replaced or discarded and the Christian elements of ritual were removed. With certain features of the ritual dropped by the new United Grand Lodge under the leadership of the Duke of Sussex, a new emulation ritual emerged, but after the Liverpool Masonic rebellion of 1823, individual lodge working gained a freedom to develop distinct flavours to their ritual, resulting in many ritualistic variations, many based on locality such as Bottomley which is found around the Liverpool area, the Humber Use found in the Hull area and of course the York and Castle Workings. The Masonic ritual has the ability to change, though with this change can comes loss. As English Freemasonry adapts to the modern period and faces lodge mergers and closures, many of these individual workings are changing and disappearing, reflecting somewhat the changes that Masonry went through before; the society being adapted, undergoing experimentation with the various rites that emerged during the eighteenth century; some dying after a number of years, some merging or later being resurrected in altered formats during the occult revival.

Notes

Foreword - pages 9-11

[1] Arturo de Hoyos, 'Masonic Rites and Systems,' in Henrik Bogdan and Jan A.M. Snoek, (eds.), *Handbook of Freemasonry*, (Leiden: Brill, 2014), pp.356-77.

[2] *<grandcollegeofrites.org>*

[3] *<latomia.org>*

Introduction - pages 13-14

[4] Lionel A Seemungal, 'The Rise of the Additional Degrees', *AQC*, Vol. 84, (1971), pp.307-312, on p.312.

Chapter 1 - pages 17-40

[5] Taken from the 'Exposition of the First Degree of the Egyptian Rite', in Henry Ridgely Evans, *Cagliostro and his Egyptian Rite*, (Washington D.C., 1919), p.25.

[6] Ibid., p.26.

[7] Arturo de Hoyos, (ed.), 'The Melissino System of Freemasonry', *Collectanea*, Vol. 23, Part 1, (Privately Printed by GCR of the USA: 2014), p.8.

[8] The Edinburgh Register House MS. (1696), supplies an early text for the ceremony of Entered Apprentice and Fellow Craft. See also David Harrison, *The Genesis of Freemasonry*, (Hersham: Lewis Masonic, 2009), pp.120-1.

[9] See David Harrison, *The York Grand Lodge*, (Bury St. Edmunds: Arima Publishing, 2014), p.33. Indeed, multiple candidates are still common in certain Masonic practices in Scotland, especially in the Mark Degree, and it is not uncommon for some Craft lodges in England to admit manageable multiple candidates, the difference today though is that the degrees are performed separately at different lodge meetings.

[10] Harrison, *Genesis of Freemasonry*, pp.116-19.

[11] Anon., *The Ancient Constitutions of the Free and Accepted Masons, with a speech deliver'd at the Grand Lodge at York*, (London: B. Creake, 1731), p.15. See also Harrison, *York Grand Lodge*, p.23.

[12] See Harrison, *Genesis of Freemasonry*, pp.88-106.

[13] David Harrison, *The Transformation of Freemasonry*, (Bury St. Edmunds: Arima Publishing, 2010), p.148.

[14] Henry Sadler, 'An Unrecorded Grand Lodge', *AQC*, Vol. 18, (1905), pp.69-90, on p.71.

[15] See John Belton, 'Brother Just One More Degree', *SRJ*, (March/April 2013), pp.7-9, on p.7.

[16] See John Yarker, *The Arcane Schools*, (Belfast: William Tait, 1909), pp.439-40.

[17] The 'Rite Ancien de Bouillon' has somewhat mysterious origins; George Oliver put forward that it had links to Chevalier Ramsay, possibly from him being on good terms with a noble family who pretended descent from the Crusader Godfrey de Bouillon. See George Oliver, *The Origin of the Royal Arch Order of Masonry*, (London: Bro. Richard Spencer, 1867), p.31. For a discussion on the Rite by Oliver, see Harrison, *Transformation of Freemasonry*, pp.147-151. A sceptical view of the Rite Ancien de Bouillon is put forward by Arturo de Hoyos in 'The Mystery of the Royal Arch Word', *Heredom*, Vol. 2, (1993), pp.7-34.

[18] John Coustos had been initiated into Freemasonry in London in 1730, and was a member of Lodge No. 75, held at the Rainbow Coffee House, London. See John Coustos, *The Sufferings of John Coustos for Free-Masonry And For His Refusing to Turn Roman Catholic in the Inquisition at Lisbon*, (London: W. Strahan, 1746), and also see John Coustos: Confession of 21 March 1743,

in S. Vatcher, 'John Coustos and the Portuguese Inquisition', *AQC,* Vol. 81, (1968), pp.50-51.
[19] Aubrey J.B. Thomas, 'A Brief History of the Royal Arch in England', *AQC*, Vol. 85, (1972), pp.349-358. See also Robert T. Bashford, 'Aspects of the History of Freemasonry in Ireland', *AQC*, Vol. 129, (2016), in which Bashford discusses the early Royal Arch in Ireland and Dassigny's book.
[20] See Belton, 'Brother Just One More Degree', *SRJ*, pp.7-9, in which Belton discusses the desire for extra degrees, a desire that dates back to the early history of Freemasonry in Britain.
[21] Arthur Edward Waite, *A New Encyclopaedia of Freemasonry*, Vol. 2, (New York: Wings Books, 1996), p.54.
[22] Ibid., p.56.
[23] Ibid., p.59.
[24] Ibid., p.61 & p.75.
[25] Ibid., p.67.
[26] Ibid., p.345.
[27] Ibid., p.275.
[28] Ibid., p.72.
[29] Ibid.
[30] Ibid., pp.275-6.
[31] Jean Baptiste Marie Ragon (1781-1862), was a French Mason, a member of the Royal Order of Scotland, and a prolific author at the time on esoteric Masonic Rites and ritual. His work *Masonerie ocultă şi iniţiere hermetică* being a notable publication in 1853. For more information on Ragon see John Songhurst, 'Ragon', *AQC*, Vol. 18, (1905), pp.97-103.
[32] See Arturo de Hoyos and Brent Morris, (Trans. & Eds.), *The Most Secret Mysteries of the High Degrees of Masonry Unveiled*, (Washington, DC: SRRS, 2011).
[33] Yarker, *Arcane Schools*, p.474.
[34] See Arturo de Hoyos, 'A 'Cocktail' from the Schröder Ritualsammlung: The Clermont System plus Additional Degrees', *Collectanea*, Vol. 16, Part 2, (Privately Printed by GCR of the USA: 1997).
[35] Yarker, *Arcane Schools*, p.474.
[36] Ibid., p.475.
[37] See Alain Bernheim and Arturo de Hoyos, 'Introduction to the Rituals of the Rite of Strict Observance', *Heredom*, Vol. 14, (2006), pp.47-104. Here, Bernheim and de Hoyos discuss the historical development of the Rite and present a translation of the first three degrees.
[38] Waite, *New Encyclopaedia of Freemasonry*, Vol. 2, pp.352-3.
[39] Ibid., pp.64-6.
[40] Friedrich Ludwig Schröder (1744-1816) was a German actor and a prominent Freemason of the period.
[41] Alain Bernheim and Arturo de Hoyos, (ed.), 'The Rite of Strict Observance', *Collectanea*, Vol. 21, (Privately Printed by GCR of the USA: 2010), pp.1-106.
[42] Ibid., p.37.
[43] Ibid., pp.85-6.
[44] For a discussion on the chivalric and Jacobite themes examined here see J. Webb, 'The Scottish Rectified Rite', *AQC*, Vol 100, (1988), pp.1-4.
[45] Waite, *New Encyclopaedia*, Vol. 2, p.353.
[46] Ibid., p.355.
[47] Ibid., p.351.
[48] Ibid.
[49] Arthur Edward Waite, *Saint-Martin the French Mystic and the Story of Modern Martinism*, (London: William Rider & Son, 1922), p.27.
[50] Yarker, *Arcane Schools*, p.470.
[51] A photograph of a copy of this charter can be seen in the book. There are many Rite de Elus Coens groups that exist today that claim to use the Pasqually ritual and celebrate this charter.
[52] Yarker, *Arcane Schools,* p.477.
[53] David Harrison, 'Thomas De Quincey: The Opium Eater and the Masonic Text', *AQC*, Vol. 129,

(2016), pp.276-281.

[54] R.A. Gilbert, 'Chaos out of Order: The Rise and Fall of the Swedenborgian Rite', *AQC*, Vol. 108, (1996), pp.122-149. See also Hamill and Gilbert, *World Freemasonry An Illustrated History*, p.69.

[55] Gilbert, 'Chaos out of Order: The Rise and Fall of the Swedenborgian Rite', *AQC*, p.123.

[56] Ibid.

[57] Arturo de Hoyas, (ed.), 'The Swedenborgian Rite', *Collectanea*, Vol. 1, No. 1, (Privately Printed by GCR of the USA: 1962), p.18.

[58] Ibid., p.17.

[59] Ibid., p.19.

[60] Ibid., p.23.

[61] Ibid., p.104.

[62] Yarker, *Arcane Schools*, p.490.

[63] Waite, *New Encyclopaedia*, Vol. 2, p.363.

[64] R.F. Gould, *History of Freemasonry*, Vol. III, (Edinburgh: T.C. Jack, 1887), p.244.

[65] See Johann Wolfgang von Goethe, *Italian Journey*, (1816-17) and Alexandre Dumas, *Mémoires D'Un Medecin. Joseph Balsamo*, (1846), both of which refer to Cagliostro.

[66] Evans, *Cagliostro and his Egyptian Rite*, pp.5-6, though Evans seems to doubt Cagliostro was Balsamo. Faulks and Cooper also reject this theory but shine little light on his mysterious origins, see Philippa Faulks and Robert L.D. Cooper, *The Masonic Magician: The Life and Death of Count Cagliostro and his Egyptian Rite*, (London: Watkins, 2008), p.1 and p.15.

[67] Waite, *New Encyclopaedia*, Vol. 1, pp.89-99.

[68] Yarker, *Arcane Schools*, p.471.

[69] See Robert Collis, 'Illuminism in the Age of Minerva: Pyotr Ivanovich Melissino (1726-1796) and High-Degree Freemasonry in Catherine the Great's Russia, 1762-1782', *Collegium, Studies Across Disciplines in the Humanities and Social Sciences*, 16, (Helsinki: Helsinki Collegium for Advanced Studies), pp.128-168.

[70] Ibid., pp.143-4. See also de Hoyos, (ed.), 'The Melissino System of Freemasonry', pp.3-4.

[71] de Hoyos, (ed.), 'The Melissino System of Freemasonry', *Collectanea*, p.4.

[72] Evans, *Cagliostro and his Egyptian Rite*, p.24.

[73] Collis, 'Illuminism in the Age of Minerva', *Collegium*, p.143.

[74] Ibid., p.147.

[75] Ibid., p.142.

[76] Waite, *New Encyclopaedia*, Vol. 1, pp.9-12.

[77] R.F. Gould, *History of Freemasonry*, Vol. III, (Edinburgh: T.C. Jack, 1887), p.244.

[78] Songhurst, 'Ragon', *AQC*, p.103. A translation of Crata Repoa by a US Mason in the early nineteenth century was also presented by Arturo de Hoyos and S. Brent Morris in their work *Committed to the Flames*, (Hersham: Lewis Masonic, 2008).

[79] See Nick Farrell, *Crata Repoa*, (Rome, 2009).

[80] Ibid., p.10.

[81] Ibid., p.14.

[82] Ibid., p.5.

[83] See Josef Wages, Reinhard Markner and Jeva Singh-Anand, *The Secret School of Wisdom; The Authentic Rituals and Doctrines of the Illuminati*, (Hersham: Lewis Masonic, 2015), pp.23-27.

[84] Ibid., pp.13-40. See also Farrell, *Crata Repoa*, pp.12-13.

[85] Waite, *New Encyclopaedia*, Vol. 1, pp.386-8.

[86] Waite, *New Encyclopaedia*, Vol. 2, pp.271-6.

[87] See de Hoyos, 'Masonic Rites and Systems', *Handbook of Freemasonry*, pp.367-8. See also Arturo de Hoyos, 'Anti-Masonic Abuse of Scottish Rite Literature', in Arturo de Hoyos (ed.), and S. Brent Morris (ed.), *Freemasonry in Context: History, Ritual, Controversy*, (Oxford: Lexington Books, 2004), pp.259-272, on p.260.

[88] Harrison, *Liverpool Masonic Rebellion and the Wigan Grand Lodge*, pp.32-3.

[89] J.M. Hamill, 'A Third Francken MS of The Rite of Perfection', *AQC*, Vol. 97, (1984), pp.200-2.

[90] Harrison, *Liverpool Masonic Rebellion and the Wigan Grand Lodge*, pp.55-8 and pp.68-9.
[91] Eustace B. Beesley, *The History of The Wigan Grand Lodge*, (Manchester: MAMR, 1920), pp.83-6.
[92] Waite, *New Encyclopaedia*, Vol. 1, pp.207-8.
[93] See Michael Hunter, 'The Enlightenment Rejection of Magic: Sceptics and their Milieux in Eighteenth-century England', Rethinking Intellectual History Keynote Address, the University of Sydney <http://sydney.edu.au/intellectual-history/documents/michael_hunter_rih_keynote.pdf> [Last accessed 4th March 2017] In the address Hunter presents how contradictory ideas of magic co-existed during the age of Enlightenment. Also see Owen Davies, *Witchcraft, Magic and Culture 1736-1951*, (Manchester: Manchester University Press, 1999), in which Davies presents a strong argument of how many different forms of magic were popular across all sections of society during the age of Enlightenment. For a contemporary essay on the criticism of superstition and religion in the age of Enlightenment, see David Hume, 'Of Miracles (1748)', *The Age of Enlightenment*, (London: The Open University, 1984), pp.47-64. Hume is also discussed, along with these themes, in Roy Porter, *Enlightenment*, (London: Penguin, 2000), pp.120-7.

Chapter 2 - pages 41-61

[94] Evans, *Cagliostro and his Egyptian Rite*, p.24.
[95] Waite, *New Encyclopaedia*, Vol. 1, p.356.
[96] Arthur Edward Waite, *Saint-Martin the French Mystic and the Story of Modern Martinism*, (London: William Rider & Son, 1922), p.16.
[97] Donald Laycock, *The Complete Enochian Dictionary*, (San Francisco: Weiser Books, 2001), p.53.
[98] Ibid., p.54.
[99] Ibid., p.63.
[100] Yarker, *Arcane Schools*, p.470-1.
[101] Waite, *Saint-Martin the French Mystic and the Story of Modern Martinism*, p.29.
[102] Ibid., pp.29-30.
[103] Ibid., pp.30-1.
[104] Ibid., p.31.
[105] Ibid., p.46.
[106] Ibid., p.43.
[107] Ibid., p.32.
[108] Ibid., p.16.
[109] Robert Ambelain, *Le Martinisme*, (Paris: 1946), Translated by Piers A. Vaughan, (2002), pp.16-18 and pp.67-73
[110] See Martin P. Starr 'Aleister Crowley: Freemason!', *AQC*, Vol. 108, (1996), pp.150-161.
[111] Evans, *Cagliostro and his Egyptian Rite*, p.14.
[112] Waite, *Saint-Martin the French Mystic and the Story of Modern Martinism*, pp.41-44. See also Louis Claude De Saint-Martin, *Des Erreurs Et De La Verite: Ou Les Hommes Rappeles Au Principe Universel De La Science*, (Lyon: A. Salomopolis, 1781).
[113] Waite, *Encyclopaedia of Freemasonry*, Vol. 2, p.338.
[114] Ibid., p.341.
[115] Waite, *Saint-Martin the French Mystic and the Story of Modern Martinism*, p.60.
[116] See Faulks and Cooper, *Masonic Magician*, p.230.
[117] Ibid.
[118] Ibid., pp.183-5.
[119] de Hoyos, 'The Melissino System of Freemasonry', *Collectanea*, pp.90-8.
[120] See Iain McCalman, 'The Making of a Libertine Queen: Jeanne de La Motte and Marie-Antoinette', *Libertine Enlightenment: Sex Liberty and Licence in the Eighteenth Century*, (Basingstoke: Palgrave Macmillan, 2003), pp.112-145, on pp.125-7.
[121] See P.D. Newman, 'Dissecting Masonic Tryptamines', *The Square*, (March, 2017), pp.22-24.

Newman's book manuscript entitled *Alchemically Stoned* is due to be published sometime in 2017.

[122] Evans, *Cagliostro and his Egyptian Rite*, pp.23-5.

[123] DMT or dimethyltryptamine is a psychedelic compound found in natural products, and can be found in various genera of acacia. See S.K. Wahba Khalil, and Y.M. Elkheir, 'Dimethyltryptamine from the Leaves of Certain Acacia Species of Northern Sudan', *Lloydia* 28, no. 2 (1975): pp.176–7.

[124] Evans, *Cagliostro and his Egyptian Rite*, p.25.

[125] Faulks and Cooper, *Masonic Magician*, p.222. The ritual was translated by the Middlesex University Translation Institute from an original MS held at the Grand Lodge of Scotland.

[126] Ibid., p.225.

[127] See Alain Gaujac, Nicola Dempster, Sandro Navickiene, Simon D. Brandt, Jailson Bittencourt de Andrade, 'Determination of *N,N*-dimethyltryptamine in beverages consumed in religious practices by headspace solid-phase microextraction followed by gas chromatography ion trap mass spectrometry', *Talanta*, Vol. 106, (2013), pp.394-398. <http://www.sciencedirect.com/science/article/pii/S0039914013000271> [Last accessed 7th December 2016]

[128] Pierre Duplais, *A Treatise on the Manufacture and Distillation of Alcoholic Liquors*, (London: Sampson Low, Son, & Marston, 1871), pp.472-3.

[129] The similarities between the wording in the Melissino System and Cagliostro's Egyptian Rite was initially brought to Newman's attention by Arturo de Hoyos, who had translated the Melissino rituals.

[130] de Hoyos, 'The Melissino System of Freemasonry', *Collectanea*, p.88. Also see Newman, 'Dissecting Masonic Tryptamines', *Square*, p.24.

[131] Arturo de Hoyas, 'Fratres Lucis', *Collectanea*, Vol. 1, Part 2, (Privately Printed by GCR of the USA: 2015), p.52.

[132] See Louise Foxcroft, *The Making of Addiction: The 'Use and Abuse' of Opium in Nineteenth Century Britain*, (London: Routledge, 2016), p.58. Foxcroft discusses how Wilde mentions opium use in his story *The Picture of Dorian Gray*, with Gray venturing into opium dens. Conan Doyle also features an opium den in his Sherlock Holmes story *The Man with the Twisted Lip*, published in 1891.

[133] See Harrison, 'Thomas De Quincey: The Opium Eater and the Masonic Text', *AQC*, pp.276-281.

[134] See Frederick Hockley, *Experimentum*, (Society of Esoteric Endeavour, 2012), which is a facsimile edition of Hockley's collected notes.

[135] See Aleister Crowley's novel *Diary of a Drug Fiend* published in 1922, which is widely believed to have been inspired by his own drug experiences.

[136] Evans, *Cagliostro and his Egyptian Rite*, p.25.

[137] See C.G. Jung, *Psychology and Alchemy*, (Hove: Routledge, 2014), p.317.

[138] Kenneth Mackenzie, *The Royal Masonic Cyclopaedia*, (Worcester: The Antiquarian Press, 1987), p.489.

[139] John Hamill, 'John Yarker: Masonic Charlatan?', *AQC*, Vol. 109, (1996), p.195.

[140] See Songhurst, 'Ragon', *AQC*, p.101. Hamill also mentions the membership of the Duke of Sussex, who apparently received the 90 degrees of Misraïm in 1821-1822, along with an authority to form a sovereign body in England. See Hamill, 'John Yarker: Masonic Charlatan?', *AQC*, p.195.

[141] See John Belton, 'Revolutionary and Socialist Fraternalism 1848-1870: London to the Italian Risorgimento', *AQC*, Vol.123, (2010), pp.231-253, on p.250.

[142] Hamill, 'John Yarker: Masonic Charlatan?', *AQC*, p.195.

[143] Waite, *New Encyclopaedia*, Vol. 2, pp.345-350.

[144] Ibid., p.348.

[145] Ibid.

[146] A.F.A., Woodford, *Kennings Cyclopaedia of Freemasonry*, (London: Kenning, 1878), p.228.

[147] Johann Reinhold Forster became a Freemason in the Lodge of Lights No. 148, in Warrington,

England, in December 1766, where Forster taught at the Warrington Dissenting Academy before taking the position on Captain Cook's second voyage. See Harrison, *Transformation of Freemasonry*, pp.23-4.

[148] de Hoyos, 'Fratres Lucis', *Collectanea*, p.4.

[149] Ibid., p.1.

[150] Ibid., p.8.

[151] Ibid., p.52.

[152] Ibid., p.19.

[153] Kenneth Mackenzie, *The Royal Masonic Cyclopaedia*, (Wellingborough: The Aquarian Press, 1987), p.611.

[154] Waite, *New Encyclopaedia*, Vol. 1, pp.353-356.

[155] de Hoyos, 'The Melissino System of Freemasonry', *Collectanea*, pp.56-8.

[156] Ibid., p.85 and p.92.

[157] Evans, *Cagliostro and his Egyptian Rite*, p.24.

[158] A.C.F. Jackson, *Rose Croix: A History of the Ancient and Accepted Rite for England and Wales*, (London: Lewis Masonic, 1980), pp.127-31.

[159] Ibid., pp.131-8.

[160] Ibid., p.161.

[161] R.S.E. Sandbach, *Priest and Freemason: the life of George Oliver*, (Wellingborough: The Aquarian Press, 1988), pp.108-109.

[162] Ibid., p.25 and pp.108-10. See also Jackson, *Rose Croix*, pp.161-75. Jackson provides an interesting and satisfactory account of not only the development of the Ancient and Accepted Rite in England and Wales, but also an interesting analysis of the development of the Rose Croix degree.

[163] Jackson, *Rose Croix*, p.170.

[164] Ibid., p.167.

[165] Arthur Edward Waite, *The Real History of the Rosicrucians*, (London: George Redway, 1887), p.415.

[166] Waite, *Saint-Martin the French Mystic and the Story of Modern Martinism*, p.21 and p.27.

[167] Arthur Edward Waite, *The Brotherhood of the Rosy Cross*, (London: William Rider & Son, 1924), quoted from Jackson, *Rose Croix*, p.30.

[168] Yarker, *Arcane Schools*, p.478.

[169] Jackson, *Rose Croix*, pp.136-7.

[170] Yarker, *Arcane Schools*, p.180.

Chapter 3 - pages 62-80

[171] Ibid., p.221.

[172] Arthur Edward Waite, *The Book of Ceremonial Magic*, (London: 1913), p.3.

[173] For a favourable discussion of Yarker's *Arcane Schools* see Hamill, 'John Yarker: Masonic Charlatan?', *AQC*, p.191 and p.198.

[174] Shepherd and Lane, *Jerusalem Preceptory No. 5, Bi-Centenary History 1786-1986*, pp.33-6.

[175] Hamill, 'John Yarker: Masonic Charlatan?', *AQC*, p.192.

[176] See Ron Greaves, *Islam in Victorian Britain: The Life and Times of Abdullah Quilliam*, (Markfield: Kube Publishing, 2010). On converting to Islam, William used the name Abdullah Quilliam.

[177] See 'The Kneph', Vol. III, No. 5, May, 1883, Yarker's journal of the Antient and Primitive Rite, where Quilliam is described as being Grand Examiner of the Grand Mystic Temple, 32-94°, Province of Lancashire.

[178] See 'The Crescent', Vol. 30, No.758, 1907, p.75. MWGM Quilliam is mentioned along with a brief report of the 33rd annual sojourn of the Ancient Order of Zuzimites, which met at the Scarisbrick Hotel in Southport, Lancashire on the 31st of July, 1907. A previous sojourn was held at Chester. The ritual for this obscure Order has been preserved in *Collectanea*, Vol. 3, Part 3, (Privately Printed by GCR of the USA: 1947).

[179] See Hugh Goddard, 'Review of Greave's Islam in Victorian Britain: The Life and Times of Abdullah Quilliam', *Yearbook of Muslims in Europe*, (2011), pp.729-31.

[180] William Abdullah Quilliam was installed Worshipful Master in the Liverpool Lodge No. 1547 on the 13th of July 1904. In the photograph of Quilliam printed in the Installation souvenir booklet, he can be seen displaying the Royal Arch and Mark Degree jewels.

[181] See for an example *The London West End Working*, (Printed for Private Circulation only, no date given), pp.147-8.

[182] Arthur Edward Waite was initiated into the London based St. Marylebone Lodge No. 1305, on the 19th of September, 1901. See also Arthur Edward Waite, *A New Encyclopaedia of Freemasonry*, Vol. I & II, (New York: Wings Books Edition, 1996) and R.A. Gilbert, 'The Masonic Career of A.E. Waite', in *AQC*, Vol. 99, (1986), pp.88-110, on p.93.

[183] See Gilbert, 'The Masonic Career of A.E. Waite', *AQC*. Also see Arthur Edward Waite, *Shadows of Life and Thought. A Retrospective Review in the Form of Memoirs* (London: Selwyn and Blount, 1938), p.162.

[184] Taken from the diary of Arthur Edward Waite, 1902/3, and quoted in Gilbert, 'The Masonic Career of A.E. Waite', *AQC*, p.95.

[185] See Waite, *Book of Ceremonial Magic*, p.184.

[186] Ibid., pp.315-18.

[187] See Joseph Fort Newton, *The Builders*, (London: George Allen & Unwin Ltd., 1924), pp.55-7. See also Gilbert, 'The Masonic Career of A.E. Waite', *AQC*, p.101.

[188] Gilbert, 'The Masonic Career of A.E. Waite', *AQC*, p.99.

[189] Ibid.,p.96.

[190] See Mary K. Greer, *Women of the Golden Dawn; Rebels and Priestesses*, (Rochester, Vermont: Park Street Press, 1995).

[191] See R.A. Gilbert, 'William Wynn Westcott and the Esoteric School of Masonic Research', *AQC*, Vol. 100, (1987), pp.6-20.

[192] Mackenzie, *Royal Masonic Cyclopaedia*, pp.vii-ix.

[193] Frederick Bligh Bond was a member of the Bristol based St. Vincent Lodge No. 1404, being initiated on the 28th of November, 1889. He served as Worshipful Master of the lodge in 1894, although his membership ceased in 1914. He was a member of the Rosicrucian Society and the infamous Ghost Club, a club which also had links to Sir Arthur Conan Doyle and occultist and Egyptologist E.A. Wallis Budge. See Frederick Bligh Bond, *The Gate of Remembrance, The story of the psychological experiment which resulted in the discovery of the Edgar Chapel at Glastonbury*, (Oxford: Oxford Blackwell, 1918). Also see Frederick Bligh Bond, *Central Somerset Gazette Illustrated Guide to Glastonbury*, (Glastonbury: Avalon Press, 1927).

[194] See Arthur Conan Doyle, *The History of Spiritualism*, (Teddington: Echo Library, 2006).

[195] See John Hamill, *The Rosicrucian Seer: The Magical Writings of Frederick Hockley*, (Wellingborough: Aquarian Press, 1986), p.15 and p.114. Also see Samuel Scarborough, 'Frederick Hockley: A Hidden Force Behind the 19th Century English Occult Revival', *JWMT*, No. 14, Vol. 2, (2008).

[196] Hamill, *The Rosicrucian Seer: The Magical Writings of Frederick Hockley*, pp.130-1.

[197] Ibid., pp.102-3.

[198] See Ellic Howe, 'Fringe Masonry in England 1870-85', *AQC*, Vol. 85, (1972), pp.242-295, on pp.251-2.

[199] Hamill, *The Rosicrucian Seer: The Magical Writings of Frederick Hockley*, pp.16-17. See also Henry Sadler, *Illustrated History of the Emulation Lodge of Improvement*, (London: Spencer & Co., 1904), p.65.

[200] See Howe, 'Fringe Masonry in England 1870-85', *AQC*, pp.262-3.

[201] Hamill, *The Rosicrucian Seer: The Magical Writings of Frederick Hockley*, p.23. See also E. Howe, *Fringe Masonry in England 1870-1885*, (Edmonds WA: Holmes Publishing Group, 1997), pp.22-3.

[202] Howe, 'Fringe Masonry in England 1870-85', *AQC*, p.271. Howe describes Cox occasionally referring to the 'Red Branch' in his correspondence with F.G. Irwin, Cox mentioning a 'final

ritual' that Irwin was due to send and that Cox was thinking of nominating members for the Order. It thus may have been an Order that Irwin and Cox revived.

[203] Ibid., p.258.

[204] Ibid., pp.257-8.

[205] Ibid., p.259. A copy of the '*Ritual of Fratris Lucis or Brethren of the Cross of Light*' in Irwin's handwriting is kept in the UGLE Library.

[206] Ibid., p.263.

[207] See John Symonds, *The Magic of Aleister Crowley*, (London: F. Muller, 1958), p.72. See also James A. Eshelman, *The Mystical and Magical System of the A.:.A.:. The Spiritual System of Aleister Crowley & George Cecil Jones Step-by-Step*, (Los Angeles: College of Thelema, 2000).

[208] Martin P. Starr, 'Aleister Crowley: Freemason!', in *AQC,* Vol. 108, (1995), pp.150-161.

[209] Waite's *The Mysteries of Magic, a Digest of the Writings of Eliphas Lévi, with a Biographical and Critical Essay*, (Redway, 1886), is discussed briefly in Gilbert, 'The Masonic Career of A.E. Waite', p.89.

[210] Hamill, 'John Yarker: Masonic Charlatan?', *AQC*, p.199.

[211] Howe, 'Fringe Masonry in England 1870-85', *AQC*, p.274.

Chapter 4 - pages 83-102

[212] F.C. Shepherd and M.P. Lane, *Jerusalem Preceptory No. 5, Bi-Centenary History 1786-1986*, (Manchester: Private Circulation, 1986), p.17.

[213] Sadler, *Illustrated History of the Emulation Lodge of Improvement*, p.4.

[214] Beesley, *Wigan Grand Lodge*, p.25.

[215] The copy of the *Old Lancashire Rituals* now on display at the Warrington Masonic Museum was transcribed by Worshipful Brother Henry White in 1863 – Past Master of the Lodge of Lights. This was once part of a private collection that belonged to West Lancashire Assistant Provincial Grand Master Ian Boswell and at the time of writing, is not listed.

[216] John Yarker, *Old Lancashire Rituals*, (1865), Grand Lodge of Iowa Library, Vault M2041 L821I.

[217] There is a manuscript ritual book with Francis George Irwin's bookplate, which has the title 'Ms. Craft lectures [copied by John Yarker from and old MS book belonging to the Lodge of Lights, Warrington]' dated c.1802, which is shelved under BE 210 CRA (item ID L15094). This copy was copied from the Yarker M.S. by Irwin, the handwriting being slightly more difficult to read than Yarker's handwriting. Yarker also made a second copy of the M.S. in 1888, which he sent to Quatuor Coronati Lodge, No. 2076. That copy is shelved under BE 210 YAR. This copy has Yarker's bookplate.

[218] See Harrison, *York Grand Lodge.*

[219] Shepherd and Lane, *Jerusalem Preceptory No. 5*, p.14.

[220] J. Armstrong, 'The Lodge of Lights No. 148', in *AQC*, Vol. 54, (1941), p.193. See also Lodge of St. John No. 322 in Lane's Masonic Records 1717-1894 <http://www.hrionline.ac.uk/lane/record.php?ID=1008> [Last accessed 21st February 2016]

[221] Herbert Woods and James Armstrong, 'A Short Historical Note on Freemasonry in Warrington', in *The By-Laws of the Lodge of Lights No. 148, Warrington*, (Warrington: John Walker & Co. Ltd., 1938), p.8. The By-Laws also includes a list of lodge members from 1765-1938.

[222] Robert Wood, *York Lodge No. 236,* (York: Published by the lodge, 1977), p.20.

[223] T.W. Hanson, *The Lodge of Probity No. 61 1738-1938*, (Halifax: Lodge of Probity, 1939), pp.189-216.

[224] *The By-Laws of the Lodge of Lights No. 148, Warrington.*

[225] The sequence of these rituals are interspersed with notes, symbols and pictures, some pages being un-numbered.

[226] John Yarker, *Old Lancashire Rituals*, p.6.

[227] Anon., *The Ritual of the Lodge of Lights No. 148*, (Warrington: Privately Published, 2015), p.18.

[228] Yarker, *Old Lancashire Rituals*, p.32 and p.35.

[229] Ibid., p.17.

[230] [William Morgan], *Illustrations in Freemasonry*, (Batavia: [New York]: 1826), p.33.

[231] Edmond Ronayne, *Handbook of Freemasonry*, (Chicago: Ezra A. Cook, 1904), p.81.
[232] Yarker, *Old Lancashire Rituals*, p.115.
[233] Ibid., p.39.
[234] Ibid., p.70.
[235] Ibid., p.109.
[236] Ibid., p.110.
[237] Morgan, *Illustrations in Freemasonry*, p.78.
[238] Yarker, *Old Lancashire Rituals*, p.80.
[239] Anon., *The Ritual of the Lodge of Lights No. 148*, (Warrington: Privately Published, 2015), p.49.
[240] Ibid, p.50.
[241] Anon., *Jachin and Boaz*, (London: W. Nicoll, 1763), p.31.
[242] Yarker, *Old Lancashire Rituals*, p.59.
[243] See Neville Barker Cryer, 'John Tunnah and the Tunnah Manuscript', *MAMR*, Vol. 100, (2010).
[244] Samuel Prichard, *Masonry Dissected*, (London: 1730), p.23.
[245] Yarker, *Old Lancashire Rituals*, p.91.
[246] Ibid., p.3.
[247] Ibid., pp.26-8.
[248] Ibid., p.16.
[249] James Anderson, *The Constitutions of the Freemasons*, (London: Senex, 1723), p.22.
[250] Christopher Powell, 'The Sheffield No. 1 MS', *AQC*, Vol. 126, (2013), pp.203-5. See also Colin Dyer 'Some Notes on the Deptford Rituals', *AQC*, Vol. 91, (1979), pp.156-167. Here, Dyer examines the Royal Arch rituals known as the Deptford Rituals (also known as the St. George MS), which date to the first few decades of the nineteenth century. Dyer also discusses the *Tunnah MS*, which contains Craft, Royal Arch and Templar rituals, which originates from the north-west of England and dates from the 1790s and, according to Dyer, has a '*close affinity*' with the St. George MS.
[251] Ibid.
[252] Hanson, *The Lodge of Probity No. 61*, p.87. Also see <http://www.westyorkskt.co.uk/page134.html> [Last accessed 24th December 2016]
[253] Wood, *York Lodge No. 236*, p.17.
[254] Neville Barker Cryer, *York Mysteries Revealed*, (Hersham: Barker Cryer, 2006), pp.446-7. See also Harrison, *York Grand Lodge*, p.73.
[255] Shepherd and Lane, *Jerusalem Preceptory No. 5*, p.60.
[256] The Prince George Lodge No. 550 was founded in 1796 but this was a Modern lodge. See Lane's Masonic Records online: <https://www.hrionline.ac.uk/lane/record.php?ID=1506> [Last accessed 31st January 2016]
[257] A number of brethren formed a new lodge using the same name after purchasing the Warrant of the Prince George Lodge in 1812. See Lane's Masonic Records online: <https://www.hrionline.ac.uk/lane/record.php?ID=1507> [Last accessed 31st January 2016]
[258] Yarker, *Old Lancashire Rituals*, un-numbered introductory page for the White Cross and Rosy Cross Section.
[259] See Richard Carlile, *Manual of Freemasonry*, (London: William Reeves, 1912), pp.306-11.
[260] Shepherd and Lane, *Jerusalem Preceptory No. 5*, p.37.

Chapter 5 - pages 103-125

[261] William Cowper, 'Table Talk', in Dr Aikin (ed.), *Select Works of the British Poets*, (London: Longman, Hurst, Rees, Orme & Brown, 1821), p.150.
[262] Carlile, *Manual of Freemasonry*, p.iv.
[263] C.F.W. Dyer, *Emulation: A Ritual to Remember*, (London: A. Lewis, 1973), p.22.
[264] See Harrison, *York Grand Lodge.*
[265] See Harrison, *Liverpool Masonic Rebellion and the Wigan Grand Lodge.*
[266] See John Hamill & R.A. Gilbert, *World Freemasonry: An illustrated History*, (London: Aquarian Press, 1991), pp.67-9.

[267] W. Wannacott, 'The Rite of Seven Degrees in London', *AQC*, Vol. 39, Part 1, (1928), pp.63-98, on p.64.

[268] See Lane's Masonic Records online <https://www.hrionline.ac.uk/lane/record.php?ID=253> [Last accessed 24th November 2016]. Wannacott believed that the Lodge of St. George de l'Observance continued to promote the additional degrees, see Wannacott, 'The Rite of Seven Degrees in London', *AQC*, p.72.

[269] Wannacott, 'The Rite of Seven Degrees in London', *AQC*, p.70.

[270] Ibid., p.71.

[271] See David S.H. Lindez, 'The Baldwyn Rite of Bristol, England', <http://www.knightstemplar.org/KnightTemplar/articles/20090822.htm> [Last accessed 20th November 2016]

[272] See Dyer, *Emulation*, pp.21-30.

[273] Hanson, *The Lodge of Probity No. 61*, pp.189-216.

[274] See P.R. James, 'The Grand-Mastership of H.R.H. The Duke of Sussex, 1813-43', The Prestonian Lecture for 1962.

[275] Sandbach, *Priest and Freemason: The Life of George Oliver*, p.99.

[276] This was certainly not uncommon; the Lodge of Probity in Halifax, Yorkshire, also has evidence that it conducted its ritual around a table during the later eighteenth century.

[277] See Harrison, *Liverpool Masonic Rebellion and the Wigan Grand Lodge*, p.59.

[278] Ibid., p.84.

[279] Ibid., pp.83-6.

[280] See Llewellyn Kitchen, (ed.), *A Ritual of Craft Masonry "Humber Use"*, (Hull: Privately Published, 1988).

[281] See Harrison, *York Grand Lodge*.

[282] See Michael Barnes, 'Spoilt for Choice', *MQ*, Issue 10, (July, 2004), <http://www.mqmagazine.co.uk/issue-10/p-62.php> [Last accessed on the 16th of January, 2012]

[283] The Merchant Lodge has its own privately printed ritual book, and has variations on the Emulation ritual.

[284] Many of these rituals can still be obtained such as Taylor's and Stability, and some are still privately printed such as the Bottomley and Humber rituals. See also Anon., *West End Ritual of Craft Masonry*, (Hersham: Lewis Masonic, 2011) and Anon., *M.M. Taylor's First Degree Handbook of Craft Freemasonry*, (Hersham: Lewis Masonic, 2006).

[285] All these rituals are still available from the Grand Lodge of Scotland.

[286] Harrison, *Transformation of Freemasonry*, pp.70-1.

[287] Carlile, *Manual of Freemasonry*, p.37.

[288] See Andrew Prescott, 'The Hidden Currents of 1813', *The Square*, Vol. 40, No. 2, (June 2014), pp.31-2. See also David Harrison, *The City of York: A Masonic Guide*, (Hersham: Lewis Masonic, 2016), p.38 and p.48.

[289] Carlile, *Manual of Freemasonry*, p.iii.

[290] See Andrew Prescott, ''The Devil's Freemason': Richard Carlile and his Manual of Freemasonry', A lecture presented to the Friends of the Library and Museum of Freemasonry, Freemason's Hall, London, 19th March, 2002.

[291] Wages, Markner and Singh-Anand, *The Secret School of Wisdom*, p.30.

[292] James Anderson, *The Constitutions of the Antient and Honourable Fraternity of Free and Accepted Masons*, (London: J. Scott, 1756), pp.189-206.

[293] Ibid., pp.218-19.

[294] Ibid., p.266.

[295] Harrison, *Liverpool Masonic Rebellion and the Wigan Grand Lodge*, p.71. There is a photograph of the Table Lodge painted by James Miller in this book.

[296] Anon., *Three Distinct Knocks*, (Dublin: Thomas Wilkinson, 1785), pp.13-14.

[297] Anon., *Jachin and Boaz*, pp.4-5.

[298] Ibid., pp.6-7.

[299] Ibid., pp.7-22.

[300] Ibid., p.29.
[301] Ibid., p.30.
[302] Neville Barker Cryer, *Masonic Hall of England: The South*, (Hersham: Lewis Masonic, 1989), p.133.
[303] The York Grand Lodge Minute Books dating from March 17, 1712 and ending August 23, 1792 are in the possession of the York 'Union' Lodge. There are no Minutes however from 1734-1761. Other York Grand Lodge relics, including furniture, jewels and the original Warrant for the Lodge of Fortitude, are all held at Freemasons Hall, Duncombe Place, York, which is the current residence of the York 'Union' Lodge No.236.
[304] Wood, *York Lodge No. 236*, p.20.
[305] Hanson, *The Lodge of Probity No.61*, p.193.
[306] The De Grey and Ripon Lodge No. 837 was constituted in October 1860 and claims to work some of the old York Working. See Harrison, *York Grand Lodge*, p.69.
[307] C.M. Browne (Compiler), *Nigerian Ritual*, (London: Lewis, 1956), p.8.
[308] *M.M. T aylor's Manual or Hand Book of Craft Freemasonry*, (London: L.J. Taylor, 1908), p.10.
[309] Browne, *Nigerian Ritual*, p.11.
[310] Anon., *Ritual of Craft Freemasonry: London West End Working*, (London: Printed for Private Circulation, Fifth Edition), p.41.
[311] *Taylor's Manual*, p.55.
[312] Anon., *The Bottomley Ritual*, (Liverpool: Privately Published for Toxteth Lodge No. 1356, 2006).
[313] Llewellyn Kitchen, (ed.), *A Ritual of Craft Masonry "Humber Use"*, (Hull: Privately Published, 1988), p.55.
[314] Anon., *Masonic Craft Ritual as used by the Royal Cumberland Lodge No. 41 from Time Immemorial*, (Bath: Privately Published by the Lodge), pp.107-8.
[315] The Memoirs of James Miller, p.13. Private Collection. Not Listed.

Chapter 6 - pages 126-145

[316] Fredric Rose, *Craft Ritual Compiled for the use of Gilbert Greenall Lodge No. 1250*, (Warrington: Privately Published, 1955). The Gilbert Greenall Lodge has recently merged with two other Warrington based lodges.
[317] Victor Hugo, *Intellectual Autobiography (Postscriptum de Ma Vie); Being the Last of the Unpublished Works and Embodying the Author's Ideas on Literature, Philosophy and Religion*, (New York: Funk & Wagnalls, 1907).
[318] Manly P. Hall, *The Secret Teachings of All Ages*, (San Francisco: H.S. Crocker & Company, 1928), p.46-7.
[319] Alexander Pope, 'Epilogue to the Satires', in *The Complete Poetical Works*, (New York: Houghton, Mifflin & Company, 1903), p.213.
[320] de Hoyos, 'The Melissino System', *Collectanea*, p.20.
[321] Bernheim and de Hoyas, 'The Rite of Strict Observance', *Collectanea*, p.95.
[322] Yarker, *Arcane Schools*, p.449-50.
[323] Philip Carter, 'The Masonic Marianne', *Pondering Freemasonry, Transactions of the Victorian Lodge of Research*, No. 218, Vol. 23, (2009), pp.47-69.
[324] Anon., *Jachin and Boaz*, (London: St. Paul's Church –Yard, 1763), p.26.
[325] Carlile, *Manual of Freemasonry*, p.307.
[326] See Ricky Pound, 'Chiswick House – A Masonic Temple?', *Brentford & Chiswick Local History Journal*, No. 16, (2007), p.5. For a discussion on Burlington's Masonic associations see Harrison, *Genesis of Freemasonry*, pp.136-7.
[327] Prince of Mercy or Scottish Trinitarian: The Twenty-Sixth Grade of the Ancient and Accepted Scottish Rite and the Eighth Degree of the Historical and Philosophical Series — *The Web of Hiram*, University of Bradford. <http://www.brad.ac.uk/webofhiram/?section=ancient_accepted&page=26princeofm.html> [Last accessed 16th February 2016]
[328] '*As Masons, we cannot appropriate to ourselves alone the lessons which this monument will teach.*

Not only to us, but to all men will it appeal.' R.W. Bro. Lawrence, D.G.M., N.Y., 1884, (regarding the Statue of Liberty), <http://www.masonicworld.com/education/articles/Masonry-and-the-statue-of-liberty.htm> [Last accessed 9th February 2016]

[329] Albert Pike, *Morals and Dogma*, (Charleston: 1871), p.379.

[330] Charles Fillmore, *Metaphysical Bible Dictionary*, (Missouri: Unity Church of Christianity, (1931), pp.69-70.

[331] Anon., *Emulation Ritual*, (Shepperton: Lewis Masonic, 1976), p.75 and p.77.

[332] Evans, *Cagliostro and his Egyptian Rite*, pp.21-2.

[333] Ibid., p.22.

[334] de Hoyos, 'The Melissino System of Freemasonry', *Collectanea*, p.10.

[335] Bernheim & de Hoyas, 'The Rite of Strict Observance', *Collectanea*, p.21.

[336] Ibid., p.92.

[337] Yarker, *Arcane Schools*, p.522.

[338] Faulks and Cooper, *Masonic Magician*, p.226.

[339] See Ricky Pound, 'Masonic Symbolism in the Red Velvet Room', *The Square*, Vol. 41, No. 4, (December, 2015), pp.61-2. The room was completed by 1730.

[340] See McCalman, 'The Making of a Libertine Queen', *Libertine Enlightenment*, p.125.

[341] Harrison, *Genesis of Freemasonry*, pp.127-8.

[342] David Harrison and Fred Lomax, *Freemasonry and Fraternal Societies*, (Hersham: Lewis Masonic, 2015), pp.99-100.

[343] Faulks and Cooper, *Masonic Magician*, p.226.

[344] Evans, *Cagliostro and his Egyptian Rite*, p.21.

[345] Harrison, *Liverpool Masonic Rebellion and the Wigan Grand Lodge*, p.63.

[346] Thomas Smith Webb, *Freemason's Monitor*, (Salam: Cushing and Appleton, 1818), pp.67-71.

[347] Ibid., p.67 and p.69.

[348] Christopher McIntosh, *Eliphas Lévi and the French Occult Revival*, (Albany: University of New York Press, 2011), pp.21-5.

[349] Harrison, *Liverpool Masonic Rebellion and the Wigan Grand Lodge*, p.63.

[350] *Royal Cumberland Lodge*, p.117.

[351] There are a number of Boys Brigade Lodges throughout England and Wales, such as the Sure and Steadfast Lodge No. 9326, which caters for ex members of the movement.

[352] Grand Master Pro Tempore, *A Charge Delivered at the Constitution of the Lodge No. CXXX at the Swan in Wolverhampton on Tuesday the 30th of October 1764*, (Birmingham: James Sketchley, 1765), p.5.

[353] See Harrison and Lomax, *Freemasonry and Fraternal Societies*, p.32 and p.112.

[354] Webb, *Freemason's Monitor*, p.69.

[355] See Basil Willey, *The Seventeenth Century Background*, (London: Chatto & Windus, 1946), pp.210-13, which discusses Sprat's notable history of the Royal Society and how the Royal Society was formed.

[356] Thaddeus Mason Harris, *Masonic Emblems Explained in a Sermon, Preached before the members of King Solomon's Lodge of Free and Accepted Masons in Charlestown, June 24, A.L. 5796*, (Boston: William Spotswood, 1796), pp.15-16.

[357] See Sir Thomas Browne, *The Garden of Cyrus*, (London: 1658). Browne concludes his work with '*All things began in order, so shall they end, and so shall they begin again*'.

[358] See Harrison, *York Grand Lodge*.

[359] Evans, *Cagliostro and his Egyptian Rite*, p.21.

[360] See McCalman, 'The Making of a Libertine Queen', *Libertine Enlightenment*, p.125.

[361] Ibid., p.127.

[362] Faulks and Cooper, *Masonic Magician*, p.12.

[363] *Constitutions of the Antient Fraternity of Free and Accepted Masons under the United Grand Lodge of England*, (London: Freemason's Hall, 1989), p.181.

[364] *A Letter from the Grand Mistress of the Female Free-Masons to Mr Harding the Printer*, (Dublin, 1724).

[365] George W. Bullimore, 'The Beehive and Freemasonry', *AQC*, Vol. 36, (1923), pp.219-33, on p.219.
[366] *Royal Cumberland Lodge Ritual*, pp.116-17.
[367] Webb, *Freemason's Monitor*, p.68.
[368] William Morgan, *Illustrations of Masonry*, p.82.
[369] See Harrison and Lomax, *Freemasonry and Fraternal Societies*, pp.32-6 and pp.99-100.

Bibliography

Ambelain, Robert, *Le Martinisme*, (Paris: 1946), Translated by Piers A. Vaughan, (2002).

Anderson, James, *The Constitutions of Freemasons*, (London: Senex, 1723).

Anon., *The Ancient Constitutions of the Free and Accepted Masons, with a speech deliver'd at the Grand Lodge at York*, (London: B. Creake, 1731).

Anon., *Jachin and Boaz*, (London: W. Nicoll, 1763).

Anon., *Three Distinct Knocks*, (Dublin: Thomas Wilkinson, 1785).

Anon., *Emulation Ritual*, (Shepperton: Lewis Masonic, 1976).

Anon., *Masonic Craft Ritual as used by the Royal Cumberland Lodge No. 41 from Time Immemorial*, (Bath: Privately Published by the Lodge, 2001).

Anon., *The Bottomley Ritual*, (Liverpool: Privately Published for Toxteth Lodge No. 1356, 2006).

Anon., *The Ritual of the Lodge of Lights No. 148*, (Warrington: Privately Published by the lodge, 2015).

Beesley, Eustace B., *The History of The Wigan Grand Lodge*, (Manchester: MAMR, 1920).

Bligh Bond, Frederick, *Central Somerset Gazette Illustrated Guide to Glastonbury*, (Glastonbury: Avalon Press, 1927).

Bligh Bond, Frederick, *The Gate of Remembrance, The story of the psychological experiment which resulted in the discovery of the Edgar Chapel at Glastonbury*, (Oxford: Oxford Blackwell, 1918).

Browne, Sir Thomas, *The Garden of Cyrus*, (London: 1658).

Butler, Alison, *Victorian Occultism and the Making of Modern Magic: Invoking Tradition*, (New York: Palgrave Macmillan, 2011).

Carlile, Richard, *Manual of Freemasonry*, (London: William Reeves, 1912)

Conan Doyle, Arthur, *The History of Spiritualism*, (Teddington: Echo Library, 2006).

Cryer, Neville Barker, *York Mysteries Revealed*, (Hersham: Barker Cryer, 2006).
Davies, Owen, *Witchcraft, Magic and Culture 1736-1951*, (Manchester: Manchester University Press, 1999).
de Hoyos, Arturo, and Morris, S. Brent, *Committed to the Flames*, (Hersham: Lewis Masonic, 2008).
de Hoyos, Arturo and Morris, Brent, (Trans. & Eds.), *The Most Secret Mysteries of the High Degrees of Masonry Unveiled*, (Washington, DC: SRRS, 2011).
Duplais, Pierre, *A Treatise on the Manufacture and Distillation of Alcoholic Liquors*, (London: Sampson Low, Son, & Marston, 1871).
Dyer, Colin F.W., *Emulation: A Ritual to Remember*, (London: A. Lewis, 1973).
Eliot, Simon, and Stern, Beverley, *The Age of Enlightenment*, (London: The Open University, 1984).
Eshelman, James A., *The Mystical and Magical System of the A.:.A.:. The Spiritual System of Aleister Crowley & George Cecil Jones Step-by-Step*, (Los Angeles: College of Thelema, 2000).
Evans, Henry Ridgely, *Cagliostro and his Egyptian Rite*, (Washington D.C., 1919).
Faulks, Philippa, and Cooper, Robert L.D., *The Masonic Magician: The Life and Times of Count Cagliostro and his Egyptian Rite*, (London: Watkins, 2008).
Foxcroft, Louise, *The Making of Addiction: The 'Use and Abuse' of Opium in Nineteenth Century Britain*, (London: Routledge, 2016).
Grand Master Pro Tempore, *A Charge Delivered at the Constitution of the Lodge No. CXXX at the Swan in Wolverhampton on Tuesday the 30th of October 1764*, (Birmingham: James Sketchley, 1765).
Greaves, Ron, *Islam in Victorian Britain: The Life and Times of Abdullah Quilliam*, (Markfield: Kube Publishing, 2010).
Greer, Mary K., *Women of the Golden Dawn; Rebels and Priestesses*, (Rochester, Vermont: Park Street Press, 1995).
Hall, Manly P., *The Secret Teachings of All Ages*, (San Francisco: H.S. Crocker & Company, 1928).
Hamill, John, *The Rosicrucian Seer: The Magical Writings of Frederick Hockley*, (Wellingborough: Aquarian Press, 1986).
Hamill, John, and Gilbert, R.A., *World Freemasonry: An Illustrated AHistory*, (London: The Aquarian Press, 1991).

Hanson, T.W., *The Lodge of Probity No. 61 1738-1938*, (Halifax: Lodge of Probity, 1939).
Harris, Thaddeus Mason, *Masonic Emblems Explained in a Sermon, Preached before the members of King Solomon's Lodge of Free and Accepted Masons in Charlestown, June 24, A.L. 5796*, (Boston: William Spotswood, 1796).
Harrison, David, *The Genesis of Freemasonry*, (Hersham: Lewis Masonic, 2009).
Harrison, David, *The Transformation of Freemasonry*, (Bury St. Edmunds: Arima Publishing, 2010).
Harrison, David, *The Liverpool Masonic Rebellion and the Wigan Grand Lodge*, (Bury St. Edmunds: Arima Publishing, 2012).
Harrison, David, *A Quick Guide to Freemasonry*, (Hersham: Lewis Masonic, 2013).
Harrison, David, *The York Grand Lodge*, (Bury St. Edmunds: Arima Publishing, 2014).
Harrison, David, and Lomax, Fred, *Freemasonry and Fraternal Societies*, (Hersham: Lewis Masonic, 2015).
Harrison, David, *The City of York: A Masonic Guide*, (Hersham: Lewis Masonic, 2016).
Hockley, Frederick, *Experimentum*, (Society of Esoteric Endeavour, 2012).
Jackson, A.C.F., Rose Croix: *A History of the Ancient and Accepted Rite for England and Wales*, (London: Lewis Masonic, 1980).
Jung, C.G., *Psychology and Alchemy*, (Hove: Routledge, 2014).
Laycock, Donald, *The Complete Enochian Dictionary*, (San Francisco: Weiser Books, 2001).
Mackenzie, Kenneth, *The Royal Masonic Cyclopaedia*, (Worcester: The Antiquarian Press, 1987).
McIntosh, Christopher, *Eliphas Lévi and the French Occult Revival*, (Albany: University of New York Press, 2011).
Morgan, William, *Illustrations in Freemasonry*, (Batavia: [New York]: 1826).
Newton, Joseph Fort, *The Builders*, (London: George Allen & Unwin Ltd., 1924).
Porter, Roy, *Enlightenment*, (London: Penguin, 2000).
Prichard, Samuel, *Masonry Dissected*, (London: 1730).
Ronayne, Edmond, *Handbook of Freemasonry*, (Chicago: Ezra A. Cook,

1904).
Sadler, Henry, *Illustrated History of the Emulation Lodge of Improvement*, (London: Spencer & Co., 1904).
Saint-Martin, Louis Claude De, *Des Erreurs Et De La Verite: Ou Les Hommes Rappeles Au Principe Universel De La Science*, (Lyon: A. Salomopolis, 1781).
Saint-Martin, Louis Claude De, *Irrthumber Und Wahrheit: Oder Ruckweiss Fur Die Menschen Auf Das Allgemeine Principium Aller Erkenntniss*, (Breslau: 1782).
Sandbach, R.S.E., *Priest and Freemason: the life of George Oliver*, (Wellingborough: The Aquarian Press, 1988).
Smith Webb, Thomas, *Freemason's Monitor*, (Salam: Cushing and Appleton, 1818).
Shepherd F.C., and Lane, M.P., *Jerusalem Preceptory No. 5, Bi-Centenary History 1786-1986*, (Manchester: Private Circulation, 1986).
Symonds, John, *The Magic of Aleister Crowley*, (London: F. Muller, 1958).
Waite, Arthur Edward, *The Real History of the Rosicrucians*, (London: George Redway, 1887).
Waite, Arthur Edward, *The Book of Ceremonial Magic*, (London: 1913).
Waite, Arthur Edward, *Saint-Martin The French Mystic And The Story of Modern Martinism*, (London: William Ryder and Son Ltd, 1922).
Waite, Arthur Edward, *Shadows of Life and Thought. A Retrospective Review in the Form of Memoirs* (London: Selwyn and Blount, 1938).
Waite, Arthur Edward, *A New Encyclopaedia of Freemasonry*, Vol. 1 & 2, (New York: Wings Books, 1996).
Willey, Basil, *The Seventeenth Century Background*, (London: Chatto & Windus, 1946).
Woods, Herbert and Armstrong, James, 'A Short Historical Note on Freemasonry in Warrington', in *The By-Laws of the Lodge of Lights No. 148, Warrington*, (Warrington: John Walker & Co. Ltd., 1938).
Wood, Robert, *York Lodge No. 236,* (York: Published by the lodge, 1977).
Woodford, A.F.A., *Kennings Cyclopaedia of Freemasonry*, (London: Kenning, 1878).
Yarker, John, *The Old Lancashire Rituals*, (1865). Grand Lodge of Iowa Library, Vault M2041 L821I.
Yarker, John, *The Arcane Schools*, (Belfast: William Tait, 1909).

Journals and Articles

Armstrong, J., 'The Lodge of Lights No. 148', in *AQC*, Vol. 54, (1941).

Barker Cryer, Neville, 'John Tunnah and the Tunnah Manuscript', *MAMR*, Vol. 100, (2010).

Bashford, Robert T., 'Aspects of the History of Freemasonry in Ireland', *AQC*, Vol. 129, (2016).

Belton, John, 'Revolutionary and Socialist Fraternalism 1848-1870: London to the Italian Risorgimento', *AQC*, Vol.123, (2010), pp.231-253.

Belton, John, 'Brother Just One More Degree', *SRJ*, (March/April 2013), pp.7-9.

Bernheim, Alain, and de Hoyos, Arturo, (ed.), 'The Rite of Strict Observance', *Collectanea*, Vol. 21, (Privately Printed by GCR of the USA: 2010).

Bullimore, George W., 'The Beehive and Freemasonry', *AQC*, Vol. 36, (1923), pp.219-233.

Carter, Philip, 'The Masonic Marianne', *Pondering Freemasonry, Transactions of the Victorian Lodge of Research*, No. 218, Vol. 23, (2009), pp.47-69.

Collis, Robert, 'Illuminism in the Age of Minerva: Pyotr Ivanovich Melissino (1726-1796) and High-Degree Freemasonry in Catherine the Great's Russia, 1762-1782', *Collegium, Studies Across Disciplines in the Humanities and Social Sciences*, 16, (Helsinki: Helsinki Collegium for Advanced Studies), pp.128-168.

de Hoyos, Arturo, (ed.), 'Ancient Order of Zuzimites', *Collectanea*, Vol. 3, Part 3, (Privately Printed by GCR of the USA: 1947).

de Hoyos, Arturo, (ed.), 'The Swedenborgian Rite', *Collectanea*, Vol. 1, No. 1, (Privately Printed by GCR of the USA: 1962).

de Hoyos, Arturo, 'The Mystery of the Royal Arch Word', *Heredom*, Vol. 2, (1993), pp.7-34.

de Hoyos, Arturo, 'A 'Cocktail' from the Schröder Ritualsammlung: The Clermont System plus Additional Degrees', *Collectanea*, Vol. 16, Part 2, (Privately Printed by GCR of the USA: 1997).

de Hoyos, Arturo, 'Anti-Masonic Abuse of Scottish Rite Literature', in Arturo de Hoyos (ed.), and S. Brent Morris (ed.), *Freemasonry in Context: History, Ritual, Controversy*, (Oxford: Lexington Books, 2004), pp.259-272.

Bernheim, Alain and de Hoyos, Arturo, 'Introduction to the Rituals of the

Rite of Strict Observance', *Heredom*, Vol. 14, (2006), pp.47-104.
de Hoyos, Arturo, 'The Melissino System of Freemasonry', *Collectanea*, Vol. 23, Part 1, (Privately Printed by GCR of the USA: 2014).
de Hoyos, Arturo, 'Masonic Rites and Systems', in Bogdan, Henrik, and Snoek, Jan A.M., (eds.), *Handbook of Freemasonry*, (Leiden: Brill, 2014), pp.355-377.
de Hoyos, Arturo, 'Fratres Lucis', *Collectanea*, Vol. 1, Part 2, (Privately Printed by GCR of the USA: 2015).
Dyer, Colin, 'Some Notes on the Deptford Rituals', *AQC*, Vol. 91, (1979), pp.156-167.
Gilbert, R.A., 'The Masonic Career of A.E. Waite', *AQC*, Vol. 99, (1986), pp.88-110.
Gilbert, R.A., 'William Wynn Westcott and the Esoteric School of Masonic Research', *AQC,* Vol. 100, (1987), pp.6-20.
Hamill, J.M., 'A Third Francken MS of The Rite of Perfection', *AQC*, Vol. 97, (1984), pp.200-202.
Hamill, John, 'John Yarker: Masonic Charlatan?', *AQC*, Vol. 109, (1996), pp.191-214.
Harrison, David, 'Thomas De Quincey: The Opium Eater and the Masonic Text', *AQC*, Vol. 129, (2016), pp.276-281.
Howe, Ellic, 'Fringe Masonry in England 1870-85', *AQC*, Vol. 85, (1972), pp.242-295.
McCalman, Iain, 'The Making of a Libertine Queen: Jeanne de La Motte and Marie-Antoinette', *Libertine Enlightenment: Sex Liberty and Licence in the Eighteenth Century*, (Basingstoke: Palgrave Macmillan, 2003), pp.112-145.
Newman, P.D., 'Dissecting Masonic Tryptamines', *The Square*, (March, 2017), pp.22-24.
Pound, Ricky, 'Chiswick House – A Masonic Temple?', *Brentford & Chiswick Local History Journal*, No. 16, (2007).
Pound, Ricky, 'Masonic Symbolism in the Red Velvet Room', *The Square*, Vol. 41, No. 4, (December, 2015), pp.61-62.
Powell, Christopher, 'The Sheffield No. 1 MS', *AQC*, Vol. 126, (2013), pp.203-205.
Scarborough, Samuel, 'Frederick Hockley: A Hidden Force Behind the 19th Century English Occult Revival', *JWMT*, No. 14, Vol. 2, (2008).
Seemungal, L.A., 'The Rise of the Additional Degrees', *AQC*, Vol. 84, (1971), pp.307-312.

Songhurst, John, 'Ragon', *AQC*, Vol. 18, (1905), pp.97-103.
Starr, Martin P., 'Aleister Crowley: Freemason!', *AQC*, Vol. 108, (1996), pp.150-161.
Wahba Khalil, S.K., and Elkheir, Y.M., 'Dimethyltryptamine from the Leaves of Certain Acacia Species of Northern Sudan', *Lloydia* 28, no. 2 (1975): pp.176–177.
Webb, J., 'The Scottish Rectified Rite', *AQC*, Vol 100, (1988), pp.1-4.

Websites

Michael Hunter, 'The Enlightenment Rejection of Magic: Sceptics and their Milieux in Eighteenth-century England', Rethinking Intellectual History Keynote Address, the University of Sydney <http://sydney.edu.au/intellectual-history/documents/michael_hunter_rih_keynote.pdf> [Last accessed 4 March 2017]

Lane's Masonic Records 1717-1894 <http://www.hrionline.ac.uk/lane/record.php?ID=1008> [Last accessed 21 February 2016]

<http://www.westyorkskt.co.uk/page134.html> [Last accessed 24 December 2016]

David S.H. Lindez, 'The Baldwyn Rite of Bristol, England', <http://www.knightstemplar.org/KnightTemplar/articles/20090822.htm> [Last accessed 20 November 2016]

The Web of Hiram, University of Bradford. <http://www.brad.ac.uk/webofhiram/?section=ancient_accepted&page=26princeofm.html> [Last accessed 16 February 2016]

R.W. Bro. Lawrence, D.G.M., N.Y., 1884, <http://www.masonicworld.com/education/articles/Masonry-and-the-statue-of-liberty.htm> [Last accessed 9 February 2016]

Index